DENIS LAW

AN AUTOBIOGRAPHY

DENIS LAW

AN AUTOBIOGRAPHY

Denis Law
in association with Ron Gubba

QUEEN ANNE PRESS
MACDONALD & JANE'S: LONDON and SYDNEY

© Denis Law and Ron Gubba 1979

First published in 1979 by
Queen Anne Press
Macdonald and Jane's Publishers Limited
Paulton House
8 Shepherdess Walk
London N1 7LW

ISBN 0354 08556 5

Photoset, printed and bound
in Great Britain by
Redwood Burn Limited
Trowbridge & Esher

CONTENTS

Foreword By Sir Matt Busby CBE

I first came across Denis Law in 1956. He was sixteen years of age at the time, and playing in Huddersfield Town's youth team against Manchester United. Even then it was obvious that the lad was something special and after the match I offered to buy him for £10,000, but Huddersfield's manager, Andy Beattie, politely but firmly turned my offer down. Two years later, when I was briefly in charge of the Scottish national side, I gave Denis his first cap at the age of eighteen. Each time I saw him I liked him more and although I was not in the bidding when he eventually went from Huddersfield to Manchester City, and then on to his Italian adventure with Torino, I did ultimately create a new British transfer market record when I paid £115,000 to bring him back from Italy. That was the most expensive signing I ever made, but on achievement he turned out to be the cheapest.

The Italians dragged me and my chairman all over Europe before we were able to complete that signing, and at one time I was so angry at the way we were being treated that I almost pulled out of the deal. I'm extremely glad now that I didn't. Once we had got Denis to Old Trafford I knew that we had the most exciting player in the game. He was the quickest thinking player I ever saw, seconds quicker than anyone else. He had the most tremendous acceleraton, and could leap to enormous heights to head the ball with almost unbelievable accuracy, and often the power of a shot. He had the courage to take on the biggest and most ferocious opponents, and his passing was impeccable. He was one of the most unselfish players I have seen. If he was not in the best position to score he would give the ball to someone who was. When a chance was on for him, even only a half chance, or in some cases no chance at all for anybody else but him, whether he had his back to goal, was sideways on, or the ball was on the deck or up at shoulder-height, he would have it in the net with such power and acrobatic agility that colleagues and opponents alike could only stand and gasp. No other player scored as many miracle goals as Denis Law. Goals which looked simple as Denis tapped them in were simple only because Denis got himself into position so quickly that opponents just could not cope with him.

He was the first British player to salaam or salute the crowd. Early on at Old Trafford the multitudes cheered him and he soon became what the crowd called him – 'The King'. He was liable to do a cross-talk act with a referee or linesman, complete with gesticulations. Some referees and some linesmen would reply in kind and make fun of it, but some were more touchy, or perhaps they would call it tougher. Certainly Denis had more than his share of trouble with referees, but it was the same very sharp reflexes, which made him the greatest man in the penalty box I ever saw, that also brought him into conflict with officialdom. Even in the ordinary scrimmaging for the ball, Denis could be spotted a mile off. With his arms and legs flailing about in a bid to get to the ball first, he looked twice as physically dangerous as he really was. It was, indeed, very often the speed of his actions rather than the actions themselves that brought him trouble, though I am not saying there were not times when he asked for all he got. On many occasions, after he had transgressed, I would say to him in the dressing room: 'When are you going to learn some sense?' And Denis would reply: 'I know that I'm wrong, and I don't want to embarrass the club, but it's no good me saying that I won't do it again. If someone kicks me I can't promise that in the heat of the moment I won't retaliate, but I will try.' His critics in this regard might not be so critical if they had seen his legs after many a game. I have seen them virtually slashed to ribbons, with blood and cuts all over the place. How much can any man stand?

Any professional football man will testify to the greatness of Denis Law, who scored more goals for Scotland than any other man, and who also scored more FA Cup goals than any other man. From personal experience, I can add that he is a good friend and a warm-hearted family man, who is never less than cheerful: an altogether nice guy who is almost as popular now with the great British sporting public as he was at the height of his career. I wish him well with his autobiography, which is typically frank and honest. Not everyone will like what they read, nor will everyone agree with some of the things he says. But football is a game which is all about opinion, everyone has his own, and this book is about a man who was one of the greatest and most talented players in the history of the game. His attitudes and opinions must be of interest to anyone who cares about football, and I commend those that do to read it.

CHAPTER 1

My First Pair of Boots

'We've decided to give you a free transfer.'

The words echoed round my brain. I was numb.

With one short sentence, Tommy Docherty had pronounced my football career dead. Could this really be the man who, only weeks earlier, had been promising me a job for life with Manchester United?

History records that I did move across town and play for a further season with Manchester City; the following summer I even went to Frankfurt as a member of Scotland's World Cup Squad and played in the match against Zaire. Not until August 1974 did I finally decide publicly to call it a day – but somehow I've always felt that the real end came on that April morning in 1973.

It was almost eighteen years to the day since I'd signed amateur forms for Huddersfield Town in April 1955. An awful lot had happened in the intervening years.

Looking back on that period now, it seems quite amazing that any of it ever happened at all. As a lad it was never my ambition to become a professional footballer – the idea simply didn't occur to me.

Of course, like all the kids in our neighbourhood, I was football daft, but football was a game that we all played – in the streets, in the school playground, anywhere we could – during every spare minute of our lives. Professional football was another world, a world with which none of us had any contact, and about which we never thought. The local team, Aberdeen, had quite a fair side in the late forties and early fifties, but I hardly ever went to see them. I was too busy playing football.

Footballers were poorly paid in those days and so I suppose that the game had little to offer in the way of a career. Boys were expected to learn a trade, and as my best subject at school was technical drawing, I had always thought I'd like to become a draughtsman. The idea of a career in football never entered my head.

When I was born on 24 February 1940 at the family home, 6 Printfield Terrace, Woodside, Aberdeen, my prospects had more connection with fishing than football.

We lived in a council-owned tenement block which housed thirty families. Mine consisted of three brothers and three sisters, in addition to mother and father. I was the youngest member of the household. My parents were honest, hard-working, but essentially poor people, typical of the area in which we lived. My father spent all of his working life on the Aberdeen trawlers, broken only by service in two world wars; with the Army in the first, and the Navy during the second.

Apart from one memory of being carried into an air-raid shelter by my sister, I don't remember the war. I was only five, and just starting school, when it ended. I do remember, though, the close-knit community spirit we had during all the years of my childhood. Because the men were always away, first with the war and later on the fishing boats, it was mainly a world of women and children.

It's funny how common hardship seems to bind people together. None of us had very much of anything, but you certainly knew that the people next door were your friends. The only time I've seen that kind of spirit in recent years was during the electricity strikes, when we were all back in the days of the blackout. Then people seemed to find the need to be neighbourly again. People help each other in adversity.

Hardship continued for most people long after the war ended. First there were food and clothing shortages, and then, when food and clothing were available again, a shortage of the money to buy them. Meat was a luxury my family rarely saw. Our meals consisted of soup and pudding; there was no middle course, and I hated soup. Well, soup's not bad, but when you start talking about four day soup . . . we only *ever* saw meat on a Sunday, and that was for my father, not the rest of us. People lived on bread and potatoes, and that was it.

As a boy I didn't have a pair of shoes until I was fourteen. Even in the bitterly cold winters when the snow was two or three feet deep with drifts six and eight feet high, I went to school in gym shoes; it was all we could afford. My mother would never apply for the free school meals, or the free boots that were available for people like us on low incomes. She was too proud.

I got my first suit when I was fifteen. Before that it was all hand-me-downs from relations, though of course we were always turned out looking clean and tidy.

In a way, I think it's a good thing to have had a deprived childhood because it makes you appreciate what you have when you finally do get on your feet. You know what you've been through and how people feel in that position. There are still people near the poverty line even today in some of the larger cities such as Glasgow, Liverpool and Manchester: not as many perhaps, but still plenty. Governments gloss over the problem, but there are people on the bread line, and I know how they feel. That is something I try to get over to my own kids, but I hope they'll never know what it's like.

Thinking back now, I marvel at how my mother managed to bring up a family of seven children on the pittance my father was able to earn going out into the North Sea doing one of the hardest jobs in the world. As late as 1958 the pay was only ten pounds a week. There were few alternative forms of employment, especially when the only trade a man knew was fishing.

Periodically the boat would be taken out about three miles to adjust the compass. This was necessary because every three months or so the compass would have lost a couple of points. Traditionally, lads from the fishing families were often taken on these short trips, and as my brothers and I grew up each of us had our turn. The trip was a chance to get some idea of the life of a trawlerman; just one such outing convinced me that it was not the life for me. A fishing trip was normally a week, but it could last for three weeks if the boat was going up to Faroes. The day I went out the weather was comparatively mild, but even so it was absolutely freezing. I could only guess at what it must be like in the depths of winter, or on a rough day when the waves could resemble mountains. On the boat, there was no heating or comfort of any kind and the crew were herded together like cattle. It's a terrible thing to think that men were obliged to accept conditions like that as normal. In addition to the discomfort, the work was back-breaking.

I'm happy to say that, like me, none of my brothers decided to follow in Dad's footsteps. Today, George has a job in a paper mill, Joe works for the railways, and John is on the buses. My sisters – Ruby, Frances and Georgina – are all married 'ladies of leisure'. Actually George, who is four years older than me, might have had a career in football. I used to watch him play for one of the Aberdeen Lads Club teams. He was a very skilful player and I'm sure that he could have been a top class professional. Unfortunately when he was eighteen he broke his leg, and that finished him as far as football was concerned.

Because my father was always away at sea, the job of bringing up the seven of us fell mostly on my mother. I didn't appreciate it at the time, but I can see now the tremendous sacrifices she had to make for us. One thing I do remember is that we were happy.

My young life revolved around playing football. There was no television then and people lived by their radio sets. All that kids did was play football in the streets. You kicked a ball against the wall all the way to school, then you had a game when you got there. At midmorning break you had another game, and you kicked a ball all the way home at lunchtime, and so it went on. The standard of schoolboy football was high and I'm sure that if the elaborate scouting systems had operated then as they do now, many more great players would have been discovered.

Things are so different today. Perhaps it's the influence of television, or maybe something else, but kids don't spend the hours playing street football the way we did, and I honestly think this has a great bearing on the lack of skill in the modern game. Most of the great players I have met developed their skills in much the same way I did. None of them learned from a textbook.

I could never get too much practice. At home we had a small kitchen with a sink, a boiler, a cooker, a gas meter, and a table where we used to eat. Above all this was a clothes rack on a pulley, which was used for airing the laundry. On winter evenings after everyone had eaten and gone into the other room, I used to clear everything off the table and suspend a ball of wool from the rack. I would then spend three or four hours at a time practising heading and kicking with either foot. I loved every minute of it.

I really believe that you can become skilled at almost anything if you practise hard enough, but you must keep at it.

*   *   *   *   *

My first experience of organised football came when I was nine years old. My mate and nextdoor neighbour, George Geddis, got me selected for the school under elevens' team. Immediately though there was a problem. I had no football boots, and without boots I couldn't play for the team. There was no way my mother could afford to buy them for me, but as luck would have it George's family, who had a bit more money than mine, had just bought him a new pair. This meant his old ones were going begging, and like the good friend that he was, George gave them to me. The crisis was averted and I made an early debut for Hilton Primary under elevens in secondhand boots; the first pair of boots I had ever owned.

It was secondhand boots for some time after that, but thanks to George Geddis I was on my way; although at that stage I still didn't know where I was going.

Today, George has a successful engineering business in Aberdeen, where he still lives. I don't see him very often, but we do meet occasionally when I'm up in Scotland.

I played for Hilton Primary for a year, then I moved to Kittybrewster School, where I played for a further year until it was time to move on to secondary school. Both school teams were successful, and I had two enjoyable years. The experience of playing for a winning team did wonders for my confidence.

Things were sailing along nicely for me, but I was in for a rude shock after I sat my eleven-plus at the end of my year at Kittybrewster. I'd been doing reasonably well academically, so well in fact that I managed to pass the exam to go to the local grammar school. No member of my family had ever been to grammar school, and I was naturally feeling quite proud of myself. The blow fell when I was told that no football was played at my new school; only rugby and cricket. I couldn't believe it. It was like the end of the world if there was to be no football.

That was it. There and then I decided that I didn't want to go to grammar school. I wouldn't go!

My mother knew how much football meant to me and agreed that if I felt so strongly then I shouldn't go. She had a terrible time trying to convince the education authorities that our decision was right. As far as they were concerned, I had passed for grammar school and I was expected to go to grammar school. Mother wrote several letters and then went to see the headmaster at Kittybrewster. She pointed out that there would be expenses for uniform and rugby and cricket kit which we couldn't afford, but our real objection was the grammar school's 'no football' status. Eventually the authorities gave in and it was agreed that I should go to Powis Secondary Modern where, as it happened, they had a number of useful football teams.

In my first year at Powis I was selected to play for Aberdeen schoolboys under twelves' team. That season we reached the final of the schoolboys' cup, and I had the thrill of playing on my first league ground. Our opponents in the final were Motherwell and Wishaw, and one leg of the two-leg tie was played at Motherwell's Fir Park Stadium. We lost on aggregate, but that was a small price to pay for the privilege of being allowed to play in such august surroundings.

At Powis I began making steady progress through the various age level teams, but I still wasn't getting enough football. When I was thirteen, a group of us joined Aberdeen Lads Club, where they already had several teams, but none for boys of our age. We decided to start our own. We needed money so George Geddis, myself and several others began going around the houses selling tickets in a football card lottery. For twopence or so, participants punched little pieces of paper bearing the names of teams out of a card, and had the chance to win ten shillings if their team was the one which was named under the seal at the top of the card. We soon established regular rounds, and as the profits rolled in we bought a set of kit and formed Aberdeen Lads Club Colts. Our fixtures were arranged for Saturday afternoons, which meant that we could play for the school in the morning and ALC in the afternoon; two games every Saturday. The team that we formed all those years ago is still in existence today.

I don't know whether or not she was prompted by my activities with ALC, but at Christmas time in 1953 my mother gave me the best present I had ever had. When I think about it now, I marvel at the sacrifice she made. Christmas for us was not a time for expensive gifts. An apple, an orange, a bag of crisps, a few peanuts and maybe a Dinky toy were the typical things we kids would be given. There was simply no money for anything else.

My father was dead against any form of credit, but in order to clothe us, unknown to father, my mother would sometimes join a credit scheme operated by three or four of the large stores in the town. The stores gave the customers a card which enabled them to spend up to an agreed amount, say ten pounds, on credit. This then had to be paid back, with interest, over a period of weeks. Mother used the system to buy essential clothing, but never for 'luxury' goods. Although I had said nothing to her, she knew exactly what I really wanted that Christmas. I'll never forget it; it was Christmas Eve and snow was falling. Mother handed me the precious card and told me to go to Clydesdale's store and buy myself a brand new pair of football boots. I had never had new football boots before in my life. I took a firm grip on that card, caught the tram, and went down to the city centre on a cloud. I bought myself a pair of Hotspur boots – I can see them now, they had big ankle protectors and were as hard as a brick, not at all like the boots of today. I can remember when I got home sitting on the sink with my feet in a basin of water to soften the leather. I could hardly believe my luck.

Those boots were cherished. They were cleaned, dried and dubbined after every match and I always made sure that they were shining again for the next game. Of course, the boots had to be hidden from my father, otherwise he would have found out about mother's credit arrangements, and he certainly would not have approved. That was the way it was. If ever I got so much as a new pair of socks, they were hidden while father was at home and they only came out again when he had gone back to sea.

Both of my parents are dead now, but I know that each in their own way did their best to give us kids a decent start in life. I don't think they did at all badly.

Children, as we all know, can be the cruellest people in the world. A kid who is unfortunate enough to be different from the rest can soon become a target for the most terrible abuse. This was something I found out the hard way. As if being poor wasn't bad enough, I inherited a family affliction which caused me no end of misery at the hands of other kids. From early childhood, all but one of my brothers and sisters had developed a squint in one eye, and from the age of five my right eye was badly crossed except when I was wearing corrective glasses. The glasses made me look pretty gawky but, without them, my eye just went straight in the corner and I looked even worse. I felt desperately self-conscious about my squint, so much so that I kept my glasses on as much as I could, even when I was playing football in the street. Every so often though the glasses would get smashed, exposing me to taunts and ridicule because of my affliction.

To make matters worse, it often took up to two months for a new pair to be made. How I suffered.

I couldn't wear glasses to play in a proper match of course, so I developed a unique system for coping with the problem. I learned to play football with one eye closed. I kept my glasses on as long as I could, while I put on my jersey and socks and boots, but when the moment came to go on to the pitch, and the glasses had to come off, I used to close my right eye and keep it closed for the whole of the match. I learned to play through an entire game using only one eye, and I went on doing this for years.

It didn't occur to me at the time, but I think that that experience probably made me tougher and more competitive. I was determined to prove that even with only one eye I was as good as anybody else. With a handicap, you had to be harder and stand up and fight, and the only way I could fight was to go on the pitch and play football. That's the way it seemed to work out anyway, as I continued to do well at Powis. In due course I graduated to Aberdeen Schoolboys under fifteen team.

Also playing for Aberdeen Schoolboys in those days were Alex Dawson, with whom I was destined to team up later in life at Manchester United; John Ogston, who went on to play in goal for Aberdeen and Scotland Under 23s; and Gordon Low, who later followed me to Huddersfield before moving on to play for Bristol City.

My highest schoolboy honour came when I was selected as reserve for Scotland Schoolboys, for an away match against Northern Ireland. It was the first time I had been out of Scotland. I watched the match from the bench. There were no substitutes then of course, but had there been I might have got on to the field for twenty minutes or so, who knows. As it was, I never did make the Scotland Schoolboys team because within weeks of that match we had an unexpected visitor at Printfield Terrace who was going to change the course of my life.

Archie Beattie was a sensible and sincere man; I learned that over the following years, but when he first called at our home, shortly before Easter in 1955, he was a complete stranger. His brother, Andy Beattie, the former Scottish international, was then manager of Huddersfield Town, and it turned out that Archie did a little scouting for the club. The purpose of his visit that day was to invite me to take part in trials in Huddersfield. Archie stressed to my mother that he didn't send boys on a wild goose chase, with the possibility of ruining their lives, and he would not be asking me to go if he didn't feel that there was a real chance of my making the grade.

Needless to say, I was overjoyed. Not because I saw myself embarking on a playing career – I didn't. Even when I eventually went to Huddersfield, I still thought I'd be back in Aberdeen inside a month; but the idea of having a trial for an English first division club was a tremendous thrill. I couldn't really believe that Huddersfield Town were likely to be very impressed by me when they saw me. After all, I was only a skinny bit of a kid weighing little more than eight stone, and I still had my squint and my owl-like glasses; although by now I did have my name down on a waiting list for an operation to correct the defect.

It didn't take long for us to decide that I should take up the offer. I was to take part in a series of trials spread over a period of four or five weeks. I was due to leave school around that time anyway, and so at Easter I said goodbye to Powis and travelled to Huddersfield accompanied by my elder brothers, John and George. It was a big departure. Apart from my father, none of our family had ever before left home. I might as well have been going to Australia. By today's standards, of course, Huddersfield was only just down the road – but then it seemed a million miles away.

In Huddersfield I was to be based at a boarding establishment called Pond House, run by a lady named Mrs Clark. I was in for another shock when I got there. I knew that there would be several other boys staying at the digs, but what I hadn't realised until I met them was that they were all English. I had never associated with English people before in my life. I was in a foreign country!

John and George stayed in Huddersfield long enough to meet Andy Beattie and to see me settled in at Mrs Clark's. All too soon though it was time for them to return home. I'll never forget that terrible feeling of loneliness as I watched their train slide out of the platform at Huddersfield station and disappear into the distance. I knew then what it meant to be homesick. I was completely alone for the first time in my life.

I must have cut a pretty forlorn figure as I made my way back across town to Pond House. The only thing that kept me going at that moment was the knowledge that I would be playing football.

CHAPTER 2

The Turning Point

Although I had gone to Huddersfield believing that I would be back home in Aberdeen in no time at all, within a few weeks of my arrival I was offered a job on the groundstaff. My wages were to be five pounds a week, and I would be able to play football for the club as an amateur. I accepted. I still couldn't see much beyond the prospect of playing for the youth team, but at least it was an opportunity to be involved in a world dominated by football, and that was sufficient.

Groundstaff duties ranged from cleaning the boots of senior players and laying out their kit for training, to cleaning the dressing rooms, sweeping the terraces, painting crash barriers, making the tea, and doing the thousand and one other jobs which crop up at a football club. I was one of a number of young lads on similar terms of employment and every afternoon, after the work was done, we had a training session. The highlights of our lives were Tuesday evening and Saturday morning, when we usually had a match.

After a tiring day, evenings were usually spent playing cards or listening to records at our digs, with an occasional visit to a cinema or the local snooker hall, but always early bed. Pond House proved to be quite comfortable. It was a large house which also provided theatrical digs for entertainers who were currently appearing in the town. I remember that Hilda Baker stayed there on one occasion.

Although I was soon reasonably settled in my new home, Huddersfield was a long way from Aberdeen, and deep down I was desperately homesick. Andy Beattie was very quick to spot this. Naturally as manager he spent most of his time looking after first team affairs, but he nevertheless did manage to keep an eye on his lads. One day not long after I arrived, he called me into his office and asked if I had a friend back in Aberdeen who was good at football and whom I might like to have join me at the club. Without hesitation I suggested Gordon Low, and sure enough, within a couple of weeks Gordon had arrived. That was how he began the career which eventually took him to Bristol City, and how, thanks to Andy Beattie's shrewdness, I overcame my loneliness and got down to starting my career. I've often wondered whether

Gordon had any regrets.

One of the things which Andy Beattie impressed on all of us was the need to keep up our studies, in case we ever needed a job outside football. He encouraged us to go to technical college in the evenings and even allowed us to take part-time jobs away from the club. Once, Gordon and I got a job working for a painting firm for a day and a half a week. They had us scraping girders and putting on coats of red lead paint, and doing all the dirty jobs that no one else wanted to do. I hated it.

I hadn't been in Huddersfield many months when something happened which was to prove a major turning point in my life. Having been on the waiting list for nearly two years, I was called into Aberdeen General Hospital to have the operation to straighten my eye.

It was a simple enough operation, which involved cutting and tightening the eye muscles. Nowadays kids have it at a much earlier age and think nothing of it, but for me, having virtually grown up with a squint, it was a very significant step. The whole business normally took about ten days, but because I caught an infection I was in hospital for three weeks.

The operation was performed by a woman doctor, and in due course the day arrived for my bandages to come off. It was just like one of those scenes from a film. The doctor carefully removed the bandages, wiped away some dried blood, and told me to go and look at myself in the bathroom mirror to see if I was satisfied with the job.

What a terrible ordeal. I had to force myself to open my eye. For anyone who hasn't been through an experience like that it may be hard to understand, but you have this terrible feeling that it won't have worked. When you've had a squint for ten years and taken endless stick from the kids as I had, it is a dreadful moment of truth. When I first looked in the mirror, I panicked. My eye was still swollen and heavily bloodshot and I thought that the operation had failed. Then I realised that the pupil was right in the centre, and that I could now open both eyes without having to look in two directions at once. It was like a miracle.

For the first time in my life that I could remember, now I could look people straight in the eye without feeling self-conscious. I would be able to go about without having to wear my glasses. I could play football without having to keep one eye closed. There would be no more persecution and name calling. It is impossible to explain exactly how much all that meant.

I've been told that I had a bit of a swagger on the football field. Well, that was the day it started. That operation completely changed my life. I strutted out of the hospital with my chest stuck out; no hurdle in life would be too great to climb from now on.

In fact I had to continue to wear my glasses for about a month, while the muscles in my eye healed, but after wearing them for ten years a further month wasn't going to be much of a hardship. Ironically, although my eye had been straightened, the vision was still badly blurred. It always has been. I still really have only one good eye. If I'd not had a normal left eye I would be virtually blind, even now. The important thing, though, was my appearance. Both eyes now looked straight ahead, and that was all that mattered. I've no doubt at all that my confidence on the field, and therefore my game, improved dramatically from that moment.

Gordon Low and I were both in the Huddersfield Town Youth Team. We played in the Northern Intermediate Youth League against teams like Leeds United and Barnsley and the rest of the Yorkshire clubs. It was a big step up from schoolboy football, and we both also had the honour of playing for the Northern Intermediate League Team.

Probably the most important game I had for the club at that time was when we met Manchester United in a round of the Youth Cup. The match was played at Heckmondwike, where if you kicked the ball too far over the touchline it ended up in the canal. Alex Dawson was in the United line-up. This was the era of the 'Busby Babes', just a couple of years before Munich, and United were the biggest name in football. We were actually beating them 2–0 at half-time, but they overran us in the second half and we lost 4–2.

I've been told that Matt Busby made a note of my name that day, and I know that around that period he made Huddersfield an offer of £10,000 for me, which Andy Beattie refused. It was a tremendous amount of money for a boy of barely sixteen, particularly when you remember that the British record transfer fee was still only in the region of £30,000. United themselves actually established a record of £45,000 when they bought Albert Quixall from Sheffield Wednesday a couple of seasons later, in 1958.

That other great Scotsman, Bill Shankly, had joined Huddersfield, and was looking after the reserve team when the club was relegated to the second division at the end of the 1955–56 season. That created some unexpected opportunities. The senior side had grown old together and was on the verge of breaking up. Several players were in their mid-thirties and reaching the end of their careers. The club had no money to buy replacements, so it had to rely on its youth. A number of reserve team players were duly promoted to the first team, and I suddenly found myself playing under Shanks in the reserves.

Compared to everything else that had so far happened to me, that was a tremendous step forward. It meant for one thing that I would now be playing on the first team pitch. Previously our matches had all been at places out in the wilds, where the ground was often two feet deep in mud and where usually there was no stand. To play at Leeds Road was by comparison almost like being given the chance to play at Hampden Park or Wembley.

As great a thrill as that was, even bigger things were to happen within a few months. By Christmas of that 1956–57 season I was an established member of the reserve team. We had just played the first of our holiday fixtures when Andy Beattie called me into his office to give me some astonishing news. I had been selected to travel to Nottingham with the first team to play in the match against Notts County on Christmas Eve. I could hardly believe it. It was less than twenty-one months since I had travelled down from Aberdeen to take part in trials, with so few expectations, and less than six months since I had graduated from the youth team to the reserves.

Thus, at the age of sixteen years and ten months, while still an amateur, I made my league debut at Meadow Lane on 24 December 1956. I played inside right, partnered on the right wing by Kevin McHale, who was only four months older than me. Together we formed one of the youngest right wing partnerships in the history of the game. I don't remember too much about the match, except that it was a very heavy muddy pitch and a gruelling game which we won 2–1. Two days later, on Boxing Day, I made my home debut in the return match against Notts County. We won that one 3–0 and I scored my first goal in league football. That season I made thirteen league appearances for Huddersfield Town and scored two goals.

Promoting me was one of the last acts of Andy Beattie's career. In January 1957 he retired and Bill Shankly took over as manager. The following month I reached my seventeenth birthday and on 25 February, one day after my birthday, Shanks signed me on professional forms for the club. The career which I had never dreamed of had come about almost as a matter of course.

Whereas Andy Beattie had been a very quiet and thoughtful man, Shanks was the complete extrovert. All he ever talked about was football, and I really mean *all* the time. He was so football minded, he used to have us playing three-a-side matches in the afternoon after we'd trained in the morning. He must have been crazy. It is hard enough with eleven-a-side on a full size pitch: imagine what it was like with three-a-side!

Shanks taught us all a lot. He would say, 'Don't work on your strengths, work on your weaknesses. Get your left foot going and get your heading going. You've got two feet and one of them isn't for standing on'. His greatest strength was his enthusiasm. He's never changed. He's grown older, but he still has the same enthusiasm for the game. He loved playing football. He gave you confidence and made you feel a bit cocky, and if you were playing well so much the better . . .

Ian St John was a typical Shankly player: a great individual with that little extra edge of cockiness. Shanks always believed that his players were the best in the world, the rest were rubbish. There really wasn't any point in playing them because you had beaten them mentally before you went on the field. Ian tells me that he was exactly the same in his days at Liverpool. At the team talk before the match he would go through the opposition man by man and tear them to shreds pointing out what he said were their weaknesses . . . for example Stepney – useless; Shay Brennan – can't kick, can't head; Dunne – can't kick with his right foot; Crerand – too slow; Foulkes – bad header; Stiles – the boy can't even see; George Best – not a bad little player but can't kick it; Bobby Charlton – no use, get tight up on him . . . and so on. It didn't matter whether the opposition were Manchester United or Real Madrid. To Shanks, compared with his team they were all rubbish. Looking at Liverpool's record over the years his technique obviously worked.

He also had an obsession about fitness. You were a professional player and you must look after yourself and keep fit. 'Be tidy, clean and healthy', he used to say. He soon decided that I needed building up. When I arrived at Huddersfield I only weighed about eight stone and he knew that to survive in football you had to have a bit of strength. He arranged with the woman who ran the cafe opposite our digs for me to be put on a diet of steaks and milk. I didn't argue about that because I'd hardly eaten meat in my life before then. Later on he had me drinking Chinese tea without sugar or milk. It was diabolical. What a character!

One thing Shanks couldn't stand was players getting injured. If you were injured you were no good to him and he didn't want to know you. He wouldn't ask 'how's the leg', or anything like that, he'd just ignore you. In those days I wasn't very strong, and the way I played I was always getting knocks and needing treatment. There was a long narrow corridor at Huddersfield where they had the boiler room, the dressing rooms, the boot room and the treatment room, with the manager's office at the other end. The corridor was so narrow that two people meeting had to struggle to get past one another. If I came out of the treatment room at the same time that Shanks was coming along the corridor, he would just walk right past me. It was incredible. Before the match I'd been the greatest player in the game, but now I'd try to catch his eye and he'd just whistle and walk past staring at the ceiling.

That happened on numerous occasions.

His other pet hate was losing. I remember once we were playing Charlton Athletic. I'd failed a fitness test before the game so I was watching the match from the front row of the stands. With twenty minutes to go we were leading 5–1 and Shanks came and sat beside me. Everything was fine. Then things began to go wrong. Charlton scored first one goal, then another. From being very confident and relaxed, he began bobbing up and down in his seat. There was no holding him. The score changed from 5–2 to 5–3, 5–4, 5–5, then with just five minutes to go, 6–5 to them. By this time Shanks was beside himself. We managed to equalise two minutes from the end and he calmed down a bit, but then, with the last kick of the match John Summers scored his fifth goal of the afternoon to make it 7–6 to them. Shanks couldn't believe it. He only saw one side and it never seemed to occur to him that Charlton had actually played very well. In the dressing room afterwards he gave our team hell.

For all his idiosyncrasies, there is no doubt that the three years at the start of my career spent playing under Bill Shankly helped me tremendously. He taught me a great deal and helped me to build one of a player's greatest assets – confidence.

It is a strange coincidence that although I came to play in England, and never played for a Scottish club, my career seemed destined to be linked with Scottish managers. Andy Beattie and Bill Shankly had got me started, and my next move would take me to play briefly under Les McDowall at Manchester City. In time I would play under Matt Busby and Tommy Docherty for Manchester United, but it was Matt who had the greatest influence on my career. In 1958, although I was still four years away from Old Trafford, he gave me one of the greatest thrills of my life: my first Scottish cap.

The 'Busby Babes' had captured the imagination of the football world in the three or four seasons before Munich, and who can possibly say what great heights might have been achieved by that team which included such players as Roger Byrne, Eddie Colman, Duncan Edwards, Tommy Taylor and the rest? Matt, of course, almost lost his own life on that dreadful day in February 1958, but he survived and, amazingly, by the early days of the following season he had not only returned to manage Manchester United, but was also manager of Scotland.

During that summer, the World Cup Finals had been held in Sweden, and Scotland had done badly finishing bottom of Group Two. One point had been taken from a 1–1 draw with Yugoslavia; the matches against Paraguay and France had been lost 3–2 and 2–1 respectively. Scottish football was at a low ebb, and people north of the border were looking to the man who had created two brilliant teams for Manchester United to perform some sort of miracle for Scotland. I wonder how many of them could have anticipated the sort of sweeping changes he would make.

The first team which Matt picked, to face Wales at Ninian Park on 18 October 1958, caused a sensation. What he did was unknown. His whole forward line was made up of Anglo-Scots, which was like a slap in the face for Scottish football.

At eighteen years and eight months, I was the youngest player to be capped for Scotland since Bob McColl in 1899, and bear in mind I was then playing for an English second division club with less than forty first team appearances to my credit. I don't believe anybody but Matt Busby would have given me a chance like that at that time.

The thing every player wants to do is to play for his country, but for me, at eighteen, after being away from home for three years it was something quite remarkable. Nothing else I ever did in football quite compared with the feeling of wearing a Scotland jersey. In all, I made fifty-five appearances for Scotland, which was a record number finally broken by Kenny Dalglish when he played in the World Cup match against Iran in 1978. I scored thirty goals for Scotland, a record which still stands.

On 18 October 1958 my thoughts were not on records. Dave Mackay missed a penalty in the first minute of the match, but as it happened it didn't matter because we won 3–0, and the record books show that I 'scored' one of the goals. What actually happened was that Dave Bowen hit a clearance against the back of my head, and it rebounded past Jack Kelsey in the Welsh goal, for just about the most bizarre goal of my career.

Scotland played well in that match, which was seen as a vindication of Matt Busby's bold selection policy. We had a very strong team with fine players like Bobby Collins at inside-forward, Jackie Henderson and Graham Leggatt on the wings, and Tommy Docherty and Dave Mackay providing great strength in mid-field. The full team was: Brown (Dundee); Grant (Hibernian); Caldow (Rangers); Mackay (Hearts), Toner (Kilmarnock), Docherty (Arsenal); Leggatt (Fulham), Collins (Everton), Herd (Arsenal), Law (Huddersfield) and Henderson (Arsenal).

Less than three weeks later the same team lined up against Northern Ireland at Hampden Park for a match which was to end in controversy for me. It was the first time I had ever played in front of a Scottish crowd, and an experience I will never forget. I have played in most of the world's great stadiums and although some of them are grander, to a Scotsman nothing compares with the experience of playing at Hampden. Unfortunately this match was to be memorable for me for some of the wrong reasons.

The danger man in the Irish line-up was their captain, Danny Blanchflower. He played deep, picking up balls from the defence and from the goalkeeper, and it was his distribution which would inspire most of the Irish attacks. Matt Busby spoke about this in the dressing room before the match, and I was given the job of marking Danny tightly, and keeping him out of the game. I took the instructions literally, and everywhere Danny went I was right beside him putting all my youthful enthusiasm into the task. On reflection, some of my tackling was probably a little *too* enthusiastic.

After the match Danny was furious, and complained bitterly that he was black and blue from head to toe. Of me he said, 'If he goes on like that, the lad won't last. He'll get himself killed'. In the light of experience, I can see now that he was right, but at the time I was simply carrying out my instructions, although I was undoubtedly doing so with a little too much zeal.

The ploy was only partially successful anyway. I did manage to keep Danny quiet for threequarters of the match, and with just over a quarter of an hour to go Scotland were leading 2–0 through goals scored by Bobby Collins and David Herd. Gradually, though, I began to tire and allowed Danny to come more into the game. They staged a tremendous fight back in which Eric Caldow turned a shot from Billy Simpson into his own net, Jimmy McIlroy knocked in the equaliser eight minutes from time, and Simpson blasted a shot against our crossbar in the dying seconds. From having been seemingly coasting to victory, in the end we were grateful to settle for a draw. All in all the result was not greeted with quite the same degree of approval as our victory over Wales had been, and I had gained something of a reputation for rough play.

Around this same period, my pal Gordon Low was named in the Scottish Under 23 squad for a match due to be played against England at Ibrox Park. Unfortunately for Gordon, the match was called off because the pitch was snowbound and by the time the next Under 23 squad was selected Gordon had lost his form and he was overlooked. Becoming an established member of the squad is an important step in international football and having so unluckily missed his opportunity, poor old Gordon never got another chance.

At the end of 1958, I twisted my knee in a league match against Charlton Athletic and then aggravated the injury a few days later in a match against Barnsley. The Huddersfield Town trainer, Roy Goodall, sent me to see a specialist and it turned out that I had split the cartilage in three places. I had an operation which kept me out of the game for two months, but I was fully recovered and back in action before the end of the season.

I missed Scotland's matches against England and West Germany through injury, but in May 1959 I went on my first international tour and played in both of our tour matches. We beat Holland 2–1 in Amsterdam, but lost 1–0 to Portugal in Lisbon a week later. In the match against Holland our inside-left, Bertie Auld, was sent off in injury time after a dust-up with the Dutch right-half Noetermans, who had been giving Bertie a hard time all afternoon.

In October we beat Northern Ireland 4–0 in Belfast, and then, six weeks later, Wales came to Hampden and took home a 1–1 draw which must have given them some satisfaction.

By the end of 1959 the wind of change was beginning to blow around Huddersfield. In his three years as manager, Shanks had built up a very useful young side. We had Ray Wilson at left-back, Gordon Low at wing-half, Les Massey and myself at inside-forward, and Kevin McHale and Mike O'Grady on the wings. As a team, we never reached our full potential because in December 1959 Shanks left to become manager of Liverpool, and with his departure the life went out of the club. Without him there was no driving force. Eddie Boot took over as manager, and as quiet a man as Andy Beattie had been, Eddie was even quieter. The moment Shanks left I knew that I would soon be on my way too. I had tasted international football now and I knew I had to go to a bigger club.

Even before Shanks's departure, my name had been linked with other clubs. Everton, Arsenal, Chelsea and Rangers were just four that were mentioned. The newspapers were full of reports suggesting that I was about to move and speculating on a new British record transfer fee in the region of £50,000. There was also quite a bit of debate in the pages of the sporting press about whether or not a lad of my limited experience could possibly be worth that amount of money. When I eventually signed for Manchester City, my playing record was eighty-one second division appearances for Huddersfield, six international appearances for Scotland, and two for Scotland Under 23s.

After he left, I thought at first that Shanks would come for me to take me to Liverpool, but he told me many years later that he hadn't because at the time Liverpool didn't have the money. As manager of Huddersfield he had turned down a bid in the region of £40,000 from Everton, so he could hardly expect now to sign me himself for less.

A few weeks after Shanks had gone, I was told to be down at the club at seven o'clock one evening because the directors were holding a board meeting to discuss offers from Arsenal and Manchester City. I didn't know where I was going, but as I rode down to the ground on the trolley bus, Arsenal were really the team on my mind. I'd said a few weeks earlier that Arsenal were the team for me and I saw no reason to change my mind. They always have been regarded as one of the best clubs in the game, and any young player would-be glad to join them.

When I got to the ground I was disappointed to find that, although Les McDowall was there for Manchester City, there was no sign of George Swindin, the Arsenal manager. I suppose in my own cheeky way I felt snubbed. If they were going to pay a record fee, I thought he ought to be there. The fact that he wasn't put me off Arsenal a bit.

I talked to Les McDowall and soon found myself fancying Manchester City. After all, they were a first division club, and that was the main attraction. I'd realised that since I had been capped and played with first division players, if I was going to get on in football then the only place to go was the first division. The fact that City were struggling badly at the time never really entered my head. I'd seen them on television in two Cup Finals, and at the time they were an attractive proposition to me. Maine Road was a lot closer to Aberdeen than London, and on reflection I didn't really want to live in London anyway. So my choice was Manchester.

The clubs agreed terms and I signed for City on 15 March 1960, for a new British record transfer fee of £55,000. Although I was not entitled to a share of the signing-on fee, Eddie Boot did promise me £300, but I never actually received a penny from the deal.

One team who hadn't been in the bidding for me was Manchester United, and a few weeks after I had signed for City I bumped into Matt Busby outside the Midland Hotel in Manchester. He told me why he hadn't tried to sign me, and his words had a prophetic ring about them.

As near as I can remember, he said, 'I would have come for you, but our team is playing particularly well at the moment. We've got Dennis Violett who is scoring a lot of goals, and there's Alex Dawson and Bobby Charlton, so there was no point in coming for you. But', he said, 'you never know'.

CHAPTER 3

The Lure of the Lira

I had moved to Maine Road in order to play first division football, but it didn't take me long to realise that City were going to have an uphill struggle to stay in the first division. I had known that they were near the foot of the league table when I joined them, but I suppose I imagined that they were just going through a bad patch, and anyway I was eager to join the first division fray. Only when I actually played for City did I appreciate the full extent of their problems.

Compared to Leeds Road, my new surroundings were magnificent. The Maine Road pitch is one of the best in the country, and everything about the club and the ground was first class; everything that is except for the kit. It was one of the first things that struck me. At Huddersfield our kit had been immaculate, we had all had our own gear marked with our initials. At City the kit was rags. It was almost as though the kit was symbolic of the team's playing performance.

My first match for them was away to Leeds United, where I scored one of the goals but we lost 4–3. I knew at once that I had joined a bad side. Apart from Bert Trautmann in goal, only Ken Barnes and George Hannah could really play. Alan Oakes was a young lad who was destined to become a very substantial player later on, but he was inexperienced at the time, and it showed. It seemed to me that the rest were either runners, or players past their best. I realised then that I was going to have to work very hard for my money, and that a great deal was expected of me personally.

City's policy in those days seemed to be to make one big signing and expect that player to do more or less everything, and of course that wasn't good enough. I had been bought to fill the gap left by Bobby Johnstone, and when I left Peter Dobing was bought to replace me. I suppose money had something to do with it – the club was trying to keep in the black – but sometimes to be successful you have to go into the red in order to get a better side. If you have a successful team, the crowds will come back and you won't be in the red for long. Only when Joe Mercer and Malcolm Allison arrived a few years later did it seem to occur to anyone at Maine Road that it takes more than one player to make a team.

Joe and Malcolm of course did buy several top class players like Colin Bell, Francis Lee, Tony Book and Mike Summerbee, and later on Rodney Marsh. They built a fine side which won the League Championship in 1968, the FA Cup in 1969, and both the League Cup and the European Cup-Winners' Cup in 1970. I often wish that I had had the chance to play in *that* City team when it was at its peak.

I played in seven matches for City at the end of the 1959–60 season and we did avoid relegation, but I knew that we had only postponed the inevitable and that the fight for survival would begin all over again in August. Normally, a team which hasn't won anything at the end of a season likes to look forward to better things to come at the start of the next season, but in City's case the outlook was negative. There was no hope. We weren't going to win anything and the start of a new season would just mean that we were back to square one. I remember thinking, 'What on earth have I joined?'

Playing problems were one thing; I soon realised that *my* problems were not going to be confined to the football field. I could not see eye to eye on training methods with our trainer, Jimmy Meadows. His ideas and mine often came into conflict and it caused quite a bit of trouble. I had enjoyed my training at Huddersfield, under Bill Shankly, and I wanted to carry on in the same way; working with a ball, practising ball control, playing five-a-sides. To me that was fabulous training and I knew that it worked. Jimmy Meadows had me on stamina training, running round and round the track, up and down the terracing, and I felt that that was no good. It was foreign to me and I didn't like it.

I rebelled, and he had me up in front of Les McDowall on many occasions about my attitude. McDowall invariably agreed with Meadows, but he never did anything about it because he knew that whatever I did at that time had to be right because I had the upper hand. I was young and I suppose I was a bit of a hot-head, but I didn't like what Meadows was doing and I wanted to have my own way. Looking back on it now, although I may have been wrong in the way I acted, there is no doubt in my mind that I was right about which were the better training methods.

By January 1961 City were again locked in a battle to steer clear of relegation, and our fortunes in the Cup were proving little better. The League Cup was in its first season and we had already been knocked out of that, 2–0, by second division Portsmouth, when we were drawn away to Cardiff in the third round of the FA Cup. Cardiff too were near the bottom of the second division; even so it took us three matches to knock them out. We finally beat them 2–0 after extra time in the second replay at Highbury. Joe Hayes and I scored the goals. It was the first FA Cup tie City had won since winning the trophy in 1956. That result brought us a fourth round tie, away to Luton, where I was destined to establish one of the game's more unusual records.

The match started in appalling conditions. It was raining heavily and the pitch was already ankle-deep in mud when we kicked off. We started badly and after eighteen minutes were trailing by 2–0. Then, in a fifteen-minute spell, I scored my first hat-trick for City to give us a 3–2 lead at half-time. It was one of those days when I couldn't put a foot wrong and in the second half I scored my second hat-trick of the match to make it 6–2 in our favour. Then, with only twenty minutes left to play, and the rain coming down in stair-rods, the referee decided to abandon the match. As we returned to Manchester that night we all had an uneasy feeling about the eventual outcome of the tie.

Ironically, when the match was replayed on the following Wednesday, conditions were actually worse than they had been on the Saturday. At least then the ball had been moving on the wet surface, now it was simply getting stuck in the mud. The fears we had had on the Saturday proved to be justified. Although I again scored a goal, we lost 3–1. I had scored seven goals in the tie and still finished up on the losing side. Somehow such a result was typical of City's fortunes at that time.

The only consolation we had when we got back on the coach was to learn that Manchester United had been beaten 7–2 at home by Sheffield Wednesday. Little did I know that eighteen months later I would be a United player.

I didn't fully appreciate the extent of the rivalry between the two clubs until I actually played in a 'derby' match. That's when I realised that the relationship between the two sets of fans wasn't friendly, by any stretch of the imagination. Ken Barnes used to say to me, 'You'll not know anything about football until you've played in a derby game. It's something completely different from anything else you've experienced'. Well, he was right, but I can't say that I ever enjoyed derby matches, and I played in more than twenty of them. That season I played in two and United won them both: 3–1 at Maine Road, and 5–1 at Old Trafford.

Something that *was* memorable from that season was the unexpected opportunity of playing for the Football League, who had previously only ever been represented by English players. In October 1960, they broke with tradition and included 'foreigners' for the first time. I had the honour of being among those selected to play against the Irish League, at Blackpool. Our team was not far short of what would have passed for a Great Britain side. We lined up as follows:

Trautmann; Angus, Armfield; Blanchflower, Adamson, Mackay; C. Jones, White, Law, McIlroy and Connelly.

Despite our vastly superior playing strength, it took us a while to master the determined Irish, but in the end we came away with a 5–2 victory and I scored two of the goals.

In March 1961 I represented the League again, this time against, of all teams, the Italian League in Milan. Within three months I was to sign for an Italian club, but the irony was not of course apparent to me then. We lost the match 4–2. Twelve months later the two teams were to meet again. This time I was playing for the Italian League, and, with an even greater touch of irony, that match was played at Old Trafford. The Italian League won again 2–0, but the most significant thing which happened to me on that occasion was a conversation I had after the match with Matt Busby. I told him how desperate I was then to get back to English football – but more of that later.

My old pal, Ken Barnes, was a reserve for the match at Blackpool, which was his only representatives honour. On a previous occasion he had been picked to play for the league in a match at Sheffield, but had broken a toe and missed the opportunity. Many people believe, and I am one of them, that Ken Barnes was the best uncapped wing-half who ever played in English football. No doubt not winning an England cap was a great disappointment to Ken, but his son Peter has since done it for him, and provided he can keep clear of injury the lad should go on to win many more caps before he is through.

Returning though to Manchester City, as the 1960–61 season drew towards its climax, we were still deep in trouble, and I was involved in two incidents which did my reputation no good.

While I was playing I always made it a policy not to go shooting my mouth off to the press. Some players like to pour out their troubles, but I always found it wiser to keep my own counsel. Always, that is, apart from the day early in 1961 when I was rash enough to say to a pressman that if City were relegated, I had no intention of returning to the second division with them. I would ask for a transfer.

To me that was merely common sense. I was an ambitious young man on my way up. I had just progressed from the second division to the first. I hadn't come to a first division club simply to step straight back into the second. I wanted to play first division football; that was my whole purpose. I didn't want to sound arrogant, or selfish. I simply thought I was being fair and honest. It didn't take long for me to realise the error of my ways. I was branded an upstart and a traitor, and it took some people a long time to forgive me. That experience taught me the wisdom of keeping my mouth shut whatever the circumstances.

In April 1961, Scotland were due to play England at Wembley and as I had played, and scored, in Scotland's previous match against Northern Ireland, I had reasonable expectations of being picked. Unfortunately, City were due to meet West Ham in a vital league match on the same day. I had never played at Wembley and I was determined not to miss the chance. Although I knew the importance of City's league match, I told Les McDowall that I wanted to play for Scotland if selected. Of course, City could have forced me to play for them, but they couldn't make me play well. Anyway they didn't try, and I was released to play for Scotland.

Thinking about that occasion now, I can see it differently. There was no real unpleasantness, but I think that if I had been manager I would have been stronger and insisted that I play for City. As it was, City achieved a 1–1 draw at West Ham.

As for my appearance at Wembley, it was a nightmare. We were annihilated 9–3. It was one of those games when everything went in. Jimmy Greaves scored a hat-trick, Bobby Smith and Johnny Haynes got two each, and Bobby Robson and Bryan Douglas each scored one. Four goals went in in one seven-minute spell towards the end of the second half. Our goals were scored by Mackay, Wilson and Quinn. It was the worst defeat in Scotland's history. Heads had to roll, and I was one of the five players dropped from Scotland's next match. Poetic justice, perhaps.

City staged a bit of a rally at the end of that season, and we actually finished in thirteenth place, although we were still only five points above Newcastle United, who were relegated along with Preston North End. Spurs had won the championship with sixty-six points and not too many points separated the teams in the bottom half of the table. I remember that in April we had home wins 2–1 against Chelsea and 4–1 against Aston Villa, and I managed to score a couple of goals in both games. Looking at our record for that season I see that we conceded ninety goals, sixty of them away from home. Our away record really was dreadful. We won only three, and drew six of our twenty-one away matches, and conceded three or more goals in twelve of them, including six each in the matches at Chelsea and West Brom. Fortunately our record at home was much better, with twenty-five points from a possible forty-two.

All in all, despite my odd problems, I had some happy days at Maine Road and I made some good friends, none more so than Ken Barnes. But the ending of that 1960–61 season also brought to an end my first spell as a Manchester City player. By now the lure of Italian football was in the air. There was a feeling that Italy was the place where it was all happening, that it was becoming the Mecca of European football. John Charles had been with Juventus for four years, but now Gigi Peronace was back in England looking for more British talent. In particular he was looking at Jimmy Greaves, but other names were being mentioned, and I was harbouring hopes that some-one might come for me. Unfortunately, Gigi had been at Wembley to witness our 9–3 thrashing so I thought that as far as he was concerned my chance must have gone.

Without doubt the really strong appeal of Italy was the money. In England the maximum wage was still only twenty pounds, although the maximum was about to be broken. Basic wages in Italy were about the same, but there were enormous bonuses to be picked up for winning. There were also very attractive signing-on fees, and a whole life-style which appeared to be far more glamorous than anything which Britain had to offer. I knew that if I stayed with City we faced the prospect of a continued fight against relegation. They were a great club, but they had a very bad team and it would take the introduction of several new players to put things right. I could see no future there at all. After more than a season fighting relegation with them, I knew that several of the team didn't try away from home, and thus the fight against relegation would go on. All of this made me decide that I wanted to go to Italy. In fact, City *were* relegated two seasons later in 1963.

A couple of weeks after Scotland's match at Wembley, I received a call from a chap who said that he was an agent for Inter Milan, who were managed at that time by Herrera. He wondered if I would be in-terested in going to Italy to play for Inter? I arranged to meet the man, and his wife, at the Midland Hotel in Manchester, and it didn't take me long to agree that I was very interested in going to Italy. The sort of money that was on offer was a signing-on fee of £5,000 plus big bonuses – £100 for a point, and £200 for winning. These were colossal figures by comparison with anything that could be earned playing football in Britain.

My contact went away to sort things out with Inter, and a few days later he turned up at my digs with the official forms for me to sign. So far, all of this had been done without the knowledge of anyone at Maine Road. I suppose I was being a bit silly, but somehow doing a deal in this rather clandestine fashion seemed to be the way one went about getting into Italian football. I signed in good faith, believing that I was agreeing to become an Inter Milan player, subject to agreement being reached between Inter and Manchester City. I somehow thought that that would all be sorted out in due course, but I knew that until the two clubs had negotiated a transfer fee, and the contract had been signed by someone from City, the deal wasn't completed. To my way of thinking I had only signed an agreement of *intent* on terms which were acceptable to me.

A few days later, Gigi Peronace appeared on the scene with an offer for me to join Torino, who had just signed Joe Baker from Hibs. The idea of joining a club with another British player, and one whom I knew, had tremendous appeal. I had only met Joe a couple of times, but I felt that I knew him reasonably well because I had been playing with his brother Gerry for Manchester City. The terms which Gigi was offering were the same as those I had been offered by Inter, and I would be signed on a two-year contract. So I decided to join Torino. As far as I was concerned, the deal with Inter had never been finally completed, although this was going to become the subject of a bitter row the moment I arrived in Italy.

Gigi negotiated a deal with City, and a transfer fee of £110,000 was agreed. It was the highest figure that had ever been paid by an Italian club for a British player, and it was exactly double what City had paid for me just over a year earlier. Nevertheless they tried hard to persuade me to stay. The maximum wage had just been abolished and Johnny Haynes, having turned down the chance of joining AC Milan, had become Britain's first £100-a-week footballer. Remember that he was the captain of England, and I was just a lad with eleven international appearances under my belt. Even so, Mr Alan Douglas, the Manchester City chairman, offered me £80 a week to stay at Maine Road. That was an awful lot of money when you consider that no one had previously earned more than £20 a week. Mr Douglas tried hard to convince me that I would not be happy in Italy but, although I was flattered by the offer, I had already made up my mind that if the chance to go to Italy came, then I was determined to take it. Thus on 6 June 1961 I signed an option to join Torino, the second Italian club for which I had signed in a matter of days.

CHAPTER 4

Survival Course

Turin is a beautiful city. Its clean, wide, tree-lined avenues are over-looked by the grand majesty of the Italian Alps. On a hill outside the city the Superga *basilica* stands in full view, a constant reminder of Italy's worst football disaster. Here in May 1949 an air-crash claimed the lives of eighteen Torino players . . . At a single stroke, the team that for four successive seasons had been the champions of Italy was wiped out. Torino Football Club has never recovered from that blow. Since that terrible day their neighbours and main rivals, Juventus, have been the premier club in Turin. Always Torino have striven to regain their lost status, and I suppose that in Joe Baker and myself some people saw fresh hope that their collective prayers might be answered. Such a responsibility was too great for two young men.

The main industry of Italy's industrial capital is the manufacture of motor cars. The large Turin Fiat factory employs most of the town's labour and, in the way that football and business are so often entwined in Italy, the powerful Agnelli brothers, who own Fiat, also run Juventus. The Italian obsession with football is well known: Italy is a Roman Catholic country, but the true religion of many of its working people is football. Support for local teams is fanatical, and the bitter rivalry between clubs is on a scale I have not experienced anywhere else in the world. Such was the background to my new life.

I actually made my first appearance in Italy, and scored my first goal on Italian soil, playing for Manchester City against Torino. Although I had signed an option to join the Italian side, a few formalities, inclu-ding a medical, still had to be completed when we flew out to play a friendly match with the club in June 1961. City were leading by that single goal when, due to torrential rain, the match was abandoned early in the second half. Before we went to Italy there was plenty of speculation in the press about my imminent move to Turin, but the formal press announcement that I had actually signed forms for Torino was made during the flight. Thus, in a way, I left Manchester a City player and arrived in Turin a Torino player. I remember feeling quite excited during the flight at the thought that when we landed I would be in my new home.

Torino are one of the few Italian clubs who actually own their own stadium. The majority of Italian teams play in stadia owned by the town. Torino's stadium was small, and unattractive, with a capacity of only 28,000. I was rather disappointed when I first saw it. I had thought that they played all their matches at the large public Stadio Comunale, but it turned out that this was only used for major matches against the likes of Juventus, Roma, or one or other of the two Milan teams. Torino Football Club was run by a board of more than a dozen directors, all of whom, I found in due course, had a different opinion on every subject under the sun. The whole operation was heavily dependent on the support of the Torino financial organisation, which had as its chairman an Argentine millionaire builder by the name of Luigi Cillario. Cillario had put up a large slice of the transfer fee which brought Joe Baker and me to Turin and, by any reckoning, he was a powerful figure in the Torino set-up.

I was greatly impressed by the warmth of the reception I received from the people of Turin. The Italians really do treat their football heroes like gods. The supporters are like a family: very friendly and very helpful. Anyone who can play at all well gets the full film star treatment. The drawback with that is that gods and film stars are public property and, as such, expected to be continually available to meet the insatiable demands of the Italian public, press, radio and television. In Italy, pressmen don't ask you to talk to them, they demand that you should.

Naturally enough, with my large transfer fee, I was big news in the Italian newspapers when I arrived; a position which didn't change much over twelve months. I enjoyed a sort of love-hate relationship with Italian journalists. On one occasion, the Italian sportswriters voted me their 'number one player', which with the likes of Charles, Suarez, Greaves and Sivori around was a very great honour. On another occasion, the sports magazine *Tutto Sport* gave me the symbolic award of a lemon for being, in their opinion, the least co-operative player. One newspaper ran a feature on me under the headline 'Valentino Law', which was a reference to Valentino Mazzola, who had been the captain and idol of the Torino team who had died in that 1949 air disaster. There really was no higher praise than that.

As soon as I set foot in Italy the newspapers were full of reports of the row between Inter and Torino, disputing to which of the two clubs I belonged. Inter were insisting that I was their player. They complained to the Italian FA and attempted to have me banned from playing for any other club. Of course, they didn't really have a leg to stand on: I knew that the contract I had signed for them was worthless without the signature of someone from Manchester City. Even so, there is so much political manoeuvring in Italian football that I suppose I was just a little bit afraid that this new stage of my career might never get off the ground.

When City returned home after the friendly match, I stayed behind to spend a few days completing formalities and meeting my new colleagues. The Italian league season was over but there were still a few outstanding fixtures, so I was able to join in a spot of training although I didn't play in a match at that time. Language was obviously going to be a problem. One or two of the Italian players spoke poor English, but that was all. I didn't speak a word of Italian, and neither did Joe Baker. (He had not yet arrived in Italy, although he had already been signed for Torino from Hibs.) During our twelve months in Turin, Joe and I depended heavily on Gigi Peronace, who acted as our interpreter and liaison man. Gigi was employed by Torino as a Sporting Director. He became a vital link between us and the club, as well as a close personal friend.

The row about which club I belonged to was still raging when the last remnants of the season ended and the players went off for their summer break. I was due to return to Scotland to see my family. Before I left, the Torino president, Angelo Filippone, assured me that by the time I returned for the start of the new season, the dispute would be settled, and so it was. By then, Inter had turned their attentions elsewhere and signed the England centre-forward, Gerry Hitchens, from Aston Villa. During the summer Jimmy Greaves had joined AC Milan, and with John Charles and Eddie Firmani already well established in Italy and Joe Baker and myself with Torino, there was quite a strong British look about the Italian League at the start of the 1961–62 season.

*   *   *   *   *

Our first match was away to Sampdoria, in Genoa, where we lost 2–0. It was August and the heat was a tremendous problem. Before the match we had trained for about six weeks and become partly accustomed to the climate, but moving south it was noticeably warmer. Genoa is actually only about a hundred miles south of Turin on the edge of the Ligurian Sea, in the northern Mediterranean. Even so, it was several degrees warmer and very humid. I remember thinking that I was dying! The sun was marvellous when you were relaxing, but it was something else to play in it. With the amount of travelling that modern clubs do, there is more awareness of such problems today, but in 1961 heat exhaustion was something I hadn't anticipated.

I knew before I went to Italy that there was a high level of skill in some of their teams, but I hadn't realised how hard the Italian game would be. Some players were extremely skilful, much more so than we had been used to back home. Those that weren't – usually defensive players – were very, very hard. They really did their job. If they were told to mark someone, they marked him. 'Never mind if you don't touch the ball, mark him.' Joe Baker and I often had two men marking each of us throughout an entire game. I was slightly more fortunate than Joe because I was able to move about a bit, but being an out-and-out striker he had to take plenty of punishment.

Kicking, punching and elbowing were all part of the game, and something not particularly physical, but which annoys British players: shirt-tugging. Just when you were going up to head a ball, your shirt would be held so that you couldn't move off the deck. Joe and I had to get used to all these things. You had to have your wits about you, particularly off the ball. You had two men marking you, and one of them was quite likely to give you a clout. It didn't matter where the ball was, it was necessary to know where the opposing centre half was all the time. It actually made us better players because we were more awake to trying to find space, continually trying to get away from an opponent, never relaxing at all. Italian teams played so defensively that there was never much space available. What there was, we had to find. We soon realised that to survive we would have to be much quicker and far more crafty than either of us had needed to be in British football.

It was tough at the time, but looking back now I'm convinced that my year in Italy made me a much sharper and better player. When I think back to the trouble I had with Danny Blanchflower at Hampden Park, I have to smile. The treatment I dished out to Danny that day was child's play compared to what went on all the time in Italian football.

Having said that Italian defenders were hard, I also felt that some of them were a bit cowardly. I certainly felt that British players were more honest. In Italy there were a lot of incidents off the ball, but if you gave them a knock back in retaliation they soon went into the Shakespearean act . . . the Old Vic on the floor.

One fairly common tactic seemed to be to try to get an opponent sent off, which happened to Joe in our very first home match. We were playing Lanerossi Vicenza and midway through the second half we were leading 3–1, with Joe having scored two of the goals and me the third. Everything was going perfectly; a dream home debut for both of us. Then the balloon went up. Joe lashed back at a fellow who had been clogging him throughout the match, and the next minute he was getting his marching orders as the real culprit did a dying swan act on the ground. The disruption which that caused in our team allowed Lanerossi to come back and score twice, to make the final score 3–3. What had looked like being a perfect day ended on a sour note, and taught us some more home truths about Italian football.

We learned something else about our Utopia as a result of that incident. It seemed that the money, which had been the main attraction in taking us to Italy, could be taken away as easily as it was given. Joe was fined £200 by the Club, and a further £100 by the FA for being sent off. He was also suspended for two matches, which meant that with lost bonuses, that one sending off cost him around £500. That was a fortune in 1961, and Joe was quite naturally furious. That was the first either of us had heard about fines, which were unknown in Britain at that time: it was one aspect of Italian football which Gigi Peronace had forgotten to mention. It didn't take us long to mention it to him, and I'm afraid we led poor Gigi a bit of a dog's life for several days following our discovery.

During the following year, we were both – Joe in particular – fined several times for various offences. Apart from being sent off, three bookings meant an automatic suspension, which in turn meant automatic fines and loss of bonuses from the matches missed. Then there were fines for breaches of club discipline, and on one occasion the whole team was fined for losing a game in Sicily. Apparently that was fairly common in Italy, although it only happened to us once. It seemed that in the money stakes it wasn't, as we had expected, all one-way traffic.

Once, Joe and I were presented with hotel bills totalling several hundred pounds after we had spent the first three months of our stay in Italy in hotel accommodation. We refused to pay on that occasion, and in time we became regular visitors at the office of Mr Guisti, the Torino Secretary, with queries about deductions from our pay. Eventually the poor man used to dread our arrival.

I never did receive the whole of my signing-on fee. I got about a third of it before I went to Italy, with the balance supposedly to be paid in two further instalments during the season. But, although I enquired about the money, I never saw it. By the time I left, I was so desperate to get away that I was glad to sacrifice what was owed, and since I never did complete my two-year contract I don't suppose I can complain too much about that – but certainly the financial rewards of playing in Italy never fully lived up to my expectations.

Having played only two games for our new club, Joe Baker and I had seen something of the other face of Italian football, and the first seeds of disillusionment had been sown. Hitchens and Suarez were also said to be having problems in Milan, where Jimmy Greaves too was finding out that life in the land of the plentiful lira was not all that it had been cracked up to be. I met Jimmy a couple of times during my travels and he was soon desperate to get back home. In fact, by late November he *was* back in England playing for Spurs. Joe and I lasted a bit more of the course, but we had problems almost every step of the way. We brought a lot of publicity to our club, and to be fair it wasn't all bad.

As a team, Torino were not much better than the Manchester City side I had just left. They had struggled to avoid relegation the previous season, and I could see that unless Joe and I could do something special we were going to have to struggle again. There were one or two promising young players, such as Vierri, our goalkeeper, who later made the Italian national side, and Ferrini, who was subsequently involved in the brawl when Italy met Chile in the World Cup Finals in Chile in 1962. Basically though, Torino was a young side with potential rather than one capable of performance. Joe Baker apart, our best players were our wing-halves, Cella and Rosato, and of course our captain, Enzo Bearzot. As you find at most clubs, the players were a great bunch of lads, and I got on particularly well with Bearzot who reminded me strongly of Ken Barnes at City. He'd been around and knew the ropes and I thought he was a great character. Many years later, of course, he became Italian national team manager and took his side to the 1978 World Cup Finals in Argentina, after beating England in the qualifying round.

After losing our opening match at Sampdoria, we had a good run of eight matches unbeaten, from which we took thirteen out of a possible sixteen points. We had a goalless draw away from home against Inter Milan. That was achievement enough, but the most significant result came when we met Juventus in our seventh match of the season. Victory for Torino over their oldest and most bitter rivals was almost as rare an occurrence as victory for Tranmere might be over Liverpool. Much therefore was expected of the new strike force of Baker and Law when the two teams met on 1 October 1961 for the first time that season. The author of *Roy of the Rovers* could not have written it better; Joe Baker scored the only goal of the game to give Torino a 1–0 victory, which sent one half of Turin mad and the other half into mourning. The match was played before a crowd in excess of 70,000 at the massive Stadio Comunale. After it was over we had to return by coach to our own stadium to collect our cars. Hours after the match, the streets were still thronged by singing and chanting crowds, and as we made our way slowly across the city we were held up by what appeared to be a funeral procession. The odd thing about it was that there seemed to be several coffins which were being carried on the shoulders of the bearers. As we got closer, we realised that the 'bearers' were actually Torino supporters and that the coffins were draped with the black and white colours of Juventus. That symbolic gesture said everything that could be said about the importance of the match result to the people of Turin.

In mid-October, Joe and I had a trip down memory lane when the whole Torino team flew into Britain for friendly matches against our two former clubs. The game at Maine Road was a bit of a fairy story for the Baker family, with Joe playing at centre forward for Torino, and his brother, Gerry, playing centre forward for Manchester City. Joe scored a hat-trick and the game was tied at 3–3 when Gerry scored a goal for City, in injury time, to make the final score 4–3 for them. Five days later we went to Scotland where we lost 2–0 to Hibs.

In between these fixtures we flew back to Italy for a league match against Atalanta, with whom we were currently sharing second place in the league table; one point behind Inter. We lost that match 2–0, which was the point at which we began to lose contact with the league championship race. After our initial run of success, things began to deteriorate. Italian league football was rubbish – totally defensive. Games were either no score, or 1–0. Rarely were more than two goals scored. When we had lost a couple of matches, we began to feel the attitude of the directors. It was as though we had lost a war. Too important! With a reaction like that, players don't want to be adventurous. Teams become stagnant at the back, nobody wants to move. Nobody wants his opposite number to get through, if he does he gets pulled down, and of course you get a lot of players playing for themselves. The game was like life and death for everybody; for the players, for the directors, for the supporters. That can't be the right way. It was not enjoyable to play, and surely not enjoyable to watch, and yet the grounds were always full: which says something about how important the game was to a lot of Italian people. Football was their whole life.

If the game itself was not much fun, one thing I did enjoy very much was the Italian system of training. It was quite different from training in Britain, and, in my opinion, very much better, the emphasis being on training for sharpness rather than stamina. In Italy a manager is normally also the coach. Our manager, Beniamino Santos, was an Argentine who had come to Torino as a striker soon after the 1949 air crash. He had only recently taken over the first team, after a spell in charge of the youth squad. He took charge of our training.

The first team squad numbered around twenty, and at the start of a session we lined up in pairs, forming two rows of ten. There was no talking, and everything was done to the whistle. Starting perhaps level with the halfway line, we would jog to one corner of the pitch, where we would pause and perform exercises to the whistle. Then we would jog to the next corner, where we would stop again to do more exercises. This was how we warmed up. It was a sharp contrast to what I had been used to in Britain, where the normal practice was to do three or four straightforward laps as a warm up. In Italy, our laps were broken up between jogging and exercises. About twenty minutes of this was normally sufficient before we moved on to our sprints and stamina training. Soon, two players – the ones considered least in need of stamina training – would be taken out and given a ball each to work on ball skills. After a while two more would be taken out, and so on, until in the end it was the biggest and heaviest men – who needed it most – who did most stamina training. Unlike the British method, where everyone tended to get the same training programme, in Italy we all had a training programme tailored to our specific needs. Our three goalkeepers trained together; the forwards would practise short sharp running; and eventually everyone ended up with a ball. I thought this was terrific, and of course, being one of the smallest, I was always one of the first to be taken out. I noticed in Argentina, in 1978, that the Italian national side was still using exactly the same methods.

Training in Italy was a real joy, but when it was over we discovered two of our biggest problems; harassment and boredom. One led to the other. In England players train in the morning and play one, or maybe two matches a week. Apart from that their time is their own. Not so in Italy, where we were subjected to continual harassment from club directors, directors of the club's financial organisation and, of course, the ordinary fans all wanting to know 'How are you feeling? Are you fit?' and so on; it never ceased. We used to have four or five thousand people watching us train, as there was no restriction on them coming in. This continual close contact which everybody had with the players was something very hard to acccept. Even after training it was hard to get away from the feeling of prying eyes watching every move. Turin has plenty of nice restaurants and cafés along its sidewalks, and I grew to love Italian food, but it was hardly ever possible to go out and have a meal in peace.

We couldn't even enjoy a couple of quiet beers. The Italians think nothing of drinking wine, they grow up with it and regard it as a normal part of everyday life. Beer drinking is something else. To be seen drinking beer is to be regarded as an alcoholic, and in no time at all someone would report us to the club and we would be carpeted before the directors for breaking club discipline. It wasn't worth all the hassle, and the result was that Joe and I hardly ever went out. Gigi actually provided us with a bodyguard, a giant of a man named Paulino, who went almost everywhere with us when we were in Turin;

but it was impossible to get away from the public gaze.

For the first three months that we were in Italy we lived in a hotel, and hardly ever went out of our room. We had the previous day's English papers to read, but apart from that it was a case of playing cards, or staring at the wall. Eventually we moved into a luxury apartment, but there we just had the same problems in more comfortable surroundings.

The apartment itself was beautiful, but we came to regard it as our prison. It was built on a hillside overlooking the river Po. You needed a key to get through the electric gates into the grounds, then there was a key and an intercom system to get through the electric door and into the block. Inside we had all the modern luxuries imaginable: marble floors with underfloor heating, two bathrooms, underground garage with connecting lift, fitted American-style kitchen, you name it we had it; but overall the place lacked a woman's touch and it was lonely. After a while Joe and I even began to get on each other's nerves.

During our first few months in Italy, we spent three or four days a week locked away in a hotel in the mountains. That was even worse, because in addition to the boredom there were always club officials watching every move. The practice, which was common in Italy, was for the team to move up to the mountains on the Wednesday and stay there, training and relaxing, until the weekend. Then, on Saturday, we would move to whichever city we happened to be playing in on the following day. The hotel was small, with about twenty bedrooms, and we simply ate and trained all day. Even the Italian lads hated it, and they were used to it. Eventually it reached the point where Joe couldn't stand it any longer and he went on hunger strike. He told Gigi that he had had enough of this crazy existence and wouldn't eat until they got him back to Turin. When the next meal-time came round Joe wasn't in his seat and Santos wanted to know where he was. Gigi had to tell him that Joe was refusing to eat. At first they pleaded with him, but it did no good. He went without food for about a day and a half. All he would say was that he didn't want to come back to the mountains ever again.

Eventually, to my amazement, they gave in and we never did return to the mountains after that trip. The rest of the players were delighted. They could hardly believe it. Even Joe and I felt that, after the mountains, returning to Turin was like going home. I am only surmising, but I can imagine that that must have caused terrible trouble between the coach and the directors. The question was bound to be asked, why were the players no longer going to the mountains? The press too would want to know. I believe there was chaos behind the scenes, but that was one of those occasions when it was better not to know what they were talking about.

It hadn't occurred to me when I went to Italy that I might have difficulty getting released to play for Scotland. The first time the problem arose was when we were due to meet Northern Ireland in Belfast at the beginning of October. In September I had been released to play in the World Cup qualifying match, against Czechoslovakia, when I'm glad to recall that I scored a couple of goals in Scotland's 3–2 victory. The Scottish FA had had to insure me for £200,000 before I was allowed to make the trip from Italy. My contract, however, only allowed for me to be released for World Cup matches, and as the match against Northern Ireland did not come into that category I was not released. The Italian league season is short, and so every game is important. The match against Northern Ireland came the day before a league match, at a time when Torino were up amongst the league leaders.

Scotland and Czechoslovakia finished joint leaders of their World Cup qualifying group, and in November we met again, in a play-off, in Brussels.

The World Cup didn't have quite the same significance in Britain then as it does now. The whole thing seems to have become far more important to us since the tournament was staged in England, and of course England won it in 1966. I've no doubt either that today's massive television coverage has created tremendous public interest, as it has done for the Olympic Games.

Possibly because the tournament wasn't taken sufficiently seriously at that time, the Scotland players who were due to meet Czechoslovakia were all playing for their respective clubs on the Saturday, five days before the international. Today those league fixtures would almost certainly be postponed, but in 1961 there was no such enlightened policy. The result was that four key players were injured and Scotland lost a large part of the body of its team. Our goalkeeper, Bill Brown, centre-half Billy McNeill, and wingers Alex Scott and Davie Wilson were all missing from the line-up in Brussels, and it is no disrespect to the players who took their places to say that Scotland were considerably weakened by their absence. Even so, we were leading 2–1 with only eleven minutes left to play when Czechoslovakia equalised with a controversial goal – similar to the one Geoff Hurst later scored for England in the 1966 World Cup Final against West Germany, where the ball bounced down from the crossbar and there was doubt about whether or not it had actually crossed the line. The match went into extra time and on the heavy, muddy pitch, the Czechs, who were a much bigger and physically stronger side than Scotland, wore us down and eventually beat us 4–2.

The following summer, in Chile, Czechoslovakia went all the way to the World Cup Final, where they were beaten 3–1 by the great Brazilian team. Would Scotland have done as well had they qualified, I wonder? We'll never know, will we?

Shortly before Christmas in 1961, I had the unforgettable experience of playing football in Sicily when Torino met Palermo in a league match. I learned later that Sivori would not play there and I can understand why. Apparently he had once been involved in an incident with a Palermo player during a match in Turin. He had been warned that when Juventus went to Sicily he would not get off the island in one piece. He never went, and I don't blame him. The place was frightening. Like a good many people, I always associate Sicily with the *mafia* – and when we arrived there a couple of days before the game, it turned out to be every bit as forbidding as I had imagined. Of an evening the streets were full of men. The atmosphere was sinister. There were no women to be seen anywhere, just men dressed in dark clothing standing around in groups of three or four. There was nothing for them to do; football seemed to be about the only form of entertainment. Even more so than in Italy, Sicily is a sharp contrast between extremes of riches and poverty. A brand new luxury hotel, such as ours, stood next door to the shanties. Being the only form of entertainment, football was everything.

When we came to play the match, the pitch was a mess. There was no grass on the surface, which was normally baked by the sun, but because it had been raining before the game, the playing area was reduced to a heap of mud. The atmosphere during the match was terrifying. I could feel the hostility on the surrounding terraces from where a constant barrage of rubbish was rained down on us.

On one occasion I went to collect a ball for a throw-in. It was just a few feet away from the high wire fence and as I looked up I gazed into a sea of evil faces which all seemed to be spitting at me. They looked just like caged animals and I'm sure that if the fence hadn't been there they would have come to get me. I remember thinking to myself, 'What the hell am I doing here?'

I was really beginning to fear for our safety when Palermo scored the only goal of the match. For once I was quite glad to finish on the losing side. I'm not sure we'd have got out the place safely had we won. As it was, our departure was still a bit hairy. The airstrip was halfway up a mountain side with a sheer drop to the sea almost immediately after take-off. As the plane banked round to fly in the direction of Rome, a gust of wind hit us and I thought for a moment that we were going down. Once we were clear of the island and heading safely back to Rome, I thought to myself 'no wonder Sivori doesn't play there'.

We were shown a glimpse of some of the ugliness surrounding

Italian football by an incident which occurred on our arrival at Rome airport. Joe and I had become friendly with a man named Mario, who was also a friend of Gigi's. Mario was a small, slightly built man who just happened to be a Juventus supporter. That night he had arranged to meet Joe and I at the airport to give us a lift into town. The team were being taken into town by coach and waiting to meet them was the chairman of the Torino financial organisation, Luigi Cillario. As I've already said, Cillario was an important man in the Torino set-up. Among other things he owned the apartment block where Joe and I lived. When he saw us talking to Mario he went mad. He told us that we shouldn't be associating with Juventus supporters and then he actually hit Mario. Joe and I were incensed, but Mario persuaded us that the best thing for us to do was to return to town in the team coach as Cillario was insisting. 'When in Rome, do as the Romans do', the saying goes, and what Cillario had done to Mario was apparently all part and parcel of the behaviour of rival Italian supporters. The men with the money virtually ruled Italian football, and in that context Cillario was a very powerful figure indeed. Ironically, he was one of the three Torino people who died the following summer, within weeks of my having returned to England. He and Santos were both killed in separate road accidents, and Signor Filippone, the club president, died from natural causes.

*   *   *   *   *

During our twelve months in Italy, Joe and I were involved in a number of well-publicised incidents. Rome was the scene of a bizarre episode the first time we went there, for a match against Roma, in the middle of November. It was an eventful match for me in which I scored a goal and missed a penalty, and we eventually drew 2–2. As it was our first visit to the Italian capital, it was agreed that the two of us could stay behind for a couple of days sightseeing, after the rest of the team had returned to Turin. Despite the time of the year, I remember that the weather was lovely and we met a girl who spoke English and arranged to have a meal with her and a friend who spoke only Italian. After the meal the two girls offered to show us round the city and they took us to the famous Via Veneto, where visiting film stars and other celebrities can usually be seen. Naturally enough we stopped for a drink at one or two of the bars and cafés along the way, but it was really all very harmless. During the course of the evening, probably because of the difficulty of one of the girls not speaking English, we changed partners, so that neither of us was accompanying the girl with whom we had started out. At the time, there seemed to be no particular significance in that switch, but the following morning Joe was all over the front pages of the Italian newspapers. They had photographed him in a variety of seemingly embarrassing situations with one of the girls. They were photographed coming out of a club, inevitably looking bleary-eyed; there was one of them leaning across the bonnet of a car; one of them swinging round a tree, Joe with his tie somewhere round the back of his neck . . . the headline in one paper read '*La Dolce Vita*' . . . The Italian press had a field day. We discovered later, after Gigi had made some enquiries, that we had been set up. One of the girls had been planted on us by a photographer and the real target had been me, but because we had changed partners they had settled for Joe. We never actually saw a photographer, they had been very slick, but of course that got us both right into hot water with Torino. The whole evening had been perfectly innocent really, but it undoubtedly looked bad and so we were fined and in disgrace.

Having made the headlines in Rome, I suppose it was inevitable that would also make a splash in Venice, when we went there to play Venezia a couple of months later. In Italy, there is always a big press and photographic session on the day before a match; after we had been through that on this occasion, Joe and I decided we would like to have a walk around the town. All we wanted was a little peace to have a stroll, and act like a couple of tourists taking in the local sights. We found ourselves being followed by a photographer and every time we turned round, there he was taking pictures. It soon began to get on our nerves, and although he didn't seem to speak English, by then we had learned sufficient Italian to make it plain that if he didn't clear off there would be trouble. Back home, no such problem would have arisen; the chap would have taken his picture and disappeared. In Italy it is different. This fellow would not be put off; he persisted. Finally, Joe lost his temper and slung a punch, which sent the fellow's glasses flying over a wall into the Grand Canal. The man himself went down on the floor with blood on his face where it had struck the pavement. In no time at all a crowd gathered and Joe and I began to walk hurriedly away. A section of the crowd followed us jabbering away in Italian and, as we turned a corner in the hope of escaping from our pursuers, we found ourselves in a cul-de-sac. By now I was beginning to panic. I could see the headlines – 'Baker in trouble again'. It nearly always was Joe, but by now anything either of us did was headlines. Eventually we did manage to push our way through the crowd, but by the time we got back to the hotel the news was all over town. Gigi knew; Santos knew; everybody knew. Santos was asking: 'What's happened now? Another incident involving Joe?' Poor old Santos!

The photographer had been taken to hospital, and soon the police arrived and we were taken down to the police station. The police took

Joe's passport, and they wanted mine even though I hadn't done anything. Then the photographer came back from the hospital with his head covered in bandages. He had no serious injuries, but what had he got which we hadn't noticed earlier? A club-foot! That was all we needed. We just hadn't noticed it. Inevitably, it was all over the front pages of the newspapers: pictures of Joe ... headlines ... there was no way Joe could play in the match, he'd have been lynched. Just think of it, a foreigner coming to town and hitting a crippled photographer. The fact that the chap had asked for it didn't matter. What should have been a run of the mill game suddenly became a war. Joe later had to pay the photographer a thousand pounds compensation, and of course he lost bonuses for missing the match. However, at the time, those of us who had to play in it had the greater problems.

To get to the ground we had to go by motor launch along the canal, passing under a great many bridges. At every one the crowds had gathered, waiting to pelt us with rubbish as we passed underneath. The game was played at a lightning pace. It was frightening; the worst I played in over there. There was no time to settle on the ball. If you did, the legs were gone. I was always associated with anything Joe did, and since he wasn't playing, I became the target. I could see them coming at me frothing at the mouth.

Before the game, Santos had said 'Don't get into any trouble; if you do there could be a riot. They could be over the wire netting'. Needless to say, we had no intention of getting into any trouble, but we didn't improve the temper of the Venetian supporters by winning the match 1–0. Travelling *to* the ground had been bad enough. Going back was far worse. Now we had added insult to injury by beating the home team. Once again, there were mobs waiting on each of the bridges. They threw everything at us, and the bombardment got so bad that we were forced to hide under the seats. It was a miracle that no one was hurt. Meanwhile, Joe Baker, the cause of all the trouble, was sitting in his hotel room watching television. I gave him a bit of stick when I got back.

By now, our lives had become a succession of controversial incidents, on and off the field, and it all seemed to have less and less to do with the game of football. Because of our reputations, opposing players were more than ever determined to keep tabs on us during a match, and because Joe and I were both rather hot-headed young men, we were often quite ready to retaliate when the going got too rough.

I remember one match in Spal, towards the end of March. It was one of the last games I played in Italy and by then my patience was just about exhausted. Although they were in the Italian first division, Spal were a very small club who, by English standards, were more like a third division side. During the match, as usual, I was being followed all over the pitch by two men, one of whom was kicking lumps out of me. I took it for as long as I could, until there was no way I was prepared to take any more. The referee was Mr Lo Bello, Italy's famous referee, who later took charge of the 1968 European Cup Final, when Manchester United beat Benfica at Wembley. I waited until he was well out of sight and the linesman was looking the other way, and I gave this fellow a tremendous crack on the jaw with my fist. He went down and out like a light. He was carried off with a faint trickle of blood oozing from the corner of his mouth. The crowd was in uproar and Mr Lo Bello, who spoke quite good English, came over to me and said, 'Denis, I didn't see what happened, but you've obviously done something. Be very careful, or you will be off!' I didn't get into any further trouble during the match, but there was trouble when it was over. As I came to go down the tunnel, there was a posse of Spal players and officials waiting for me. They rained blows on me from all sides and I needed the assistance of one or two of the Torino players to get to the dressing room safely. It was a pretty ugly scene, with several scuffles going on in the tunnel.

Events like these were commonplace on Italian football grounds and we were involved in our share of them, but by far the most serious episode during the twelve months we were in Italy was a car accident in Turin on 7 February 1962. That very nearly cost Joe Baker and me our lives.

My brother, Joe, had come to stay with us for a few days round about the time that Joe Baker had taken delivery of a brand new motor car; an Alfa Romeo Julietta Sprint, a beautiful car. Up to that time we had been using a Fiat 600, which was provided by the club, and I had done most of the driving. Joe was not too familiar with driving in Italy, but naturally enough, having bought the new car, he wanted to drive it.

We called at a restaurant up in the mountains, where we had a light meal and a few drinks, but we were certainly not drunk, as some of the papers suggested the following day. After the meal it was still early, and we decided to drive back to Turin to visit a place where we had discovered it was possible to get a quiet drink and a little entertainment without too much fuss. It was around midnight when we got back to the city, and I remember that it had been raining, so the streets were wet. We came to a roundabout, which had a very deep kerb. Because he hadn't done much driving in Italy, Joe wasn't used to driving on the right, and he instinctively started to drive round it the British way. I said, 'Joe, you're going round the wrong way'. As soon as he realised what he was doing he pulled the car round, which was the last thing I remembered until I woke up in hospital. We realised later that the wheel must have struck the high kerb and the car was spun over. I believe that we did three or four somersaults and came to rest two or three feet from a telegraph pole. We hadn't been going particularly fast, and had the kerb been a normal height we would probably have just gone over it. As it was we came within an inch of extinction.

Joe had been thrown out on to the road and took the full impact on his face. I had been flung out of my own seat into Joe's, and where I had been sitting the car's roof was flattened level with the dashboard. Had I remained in my seat I would certainly have been dead. My brother Joe had been sitting in the back, where there wasn't a proper seat, and ironically he didn't have a scratch. I had a slight cut on my left hand which required a stitch; a year later, after always having pain there, I pulled out a quarter-inch long sliver of glass which the hospital staff had apparently missed. Perhaps that was because they were so busy looking after Joe Baker. His injuries were hideous. In addition to smashing his nose and his cheekbone, he had also split his palate, so that the roof of his mouth had dropped. It had to be sewn back into place. He was having emergency operations all through the night, and when I saw him the following day I could hardly believe it. He was inside an oxygen tent with a drip feed and bottle of plasma, looking just like the invisible man. His head was completely swathed in bandages with just a couple of holes for his eyes. They had had to bore a hole in his neck so that he could breath. When I saw him like that I felt certain he was going to die. In fact he was on the critical list for three days, and the doctors said that had he not been a footballer, and extremely fit and strong, he would not have survived. As it was he went without solid food, living only on the drip, for forty-two days.

After the hospital had stitched my hand, I was sent home to sleep it off. The following morning the first visitor who came to the flat to see how we were was John Charles. Over the months, John had become a good friend to us. Several times he had taken us out either to his home or to his restaurant for a meal. Unlike us, he had settled down well in Italy. He played for the top team, Juventus, and the crowd idolised him and called him 'the King'. His first question to me that morning was 'What the hell have you two buggers been up to now?' Having lived there for five years, John could read Italian and he brought with him a stack of Italian newspapers, so he was able to translate for me what the Italian press was making of this latest episode. To them it was all the result of a drunken orgy. There were pictures of the wrecked car on all the front pages. It was a write-off. When I saw the crushed roof on the side where I had been sitting, I realised how close I had come to being killed. I have often thought since then that had I been strapped in by a seat belt I *would* have been killed. When I saw the state Joe was in at the hospital later in the day, I realised how close we had both come to death. Actually, when he regained consciousness, Joe was convinced that I was dead and Gigi Peronace had to take me to see him to prove to him that I really was alive.

That near catastrophe virtually brought to an end the Torino playing partnership of Baker and Law. By the time Joe returned to the team, at the end of April, I was playing my last match for the club, although I didn't realise it at the time. Joe's stay in hospital had been a big loss to the team, and our form had suffered. It had also been a big loss to me personally, because while Joe was away I had been living on my own at the apartment and things had become desperate. I had had enough: enough of the boredom; enough of the continual harassment by press and public alike; enough of the rough, negative football; enough of the continual bickering and petty squabbling which are all part of Italian football. It was an existence with never a moment's real peace.

I told Torino that I was through and that I wanted to end my contract and get back to England, although at first I don't think they really took me seriously. Matters finally reached a head when we met second division Naples in the quarter final of the Italian FA Cup on 25 April 1962.

Scotland were due to play Uruguay in a friendly at the beginning of May, and I was hoping to play in that match. A few weeks earlier I had played against England at Hampden Park in match which Scotland won 2–0. I was not, however, destined to play against Uruguay.

The Italian Cup competition is not taken very seriously. It's a non-event, a fact which can be gauged from the attendance of around 5,000 for our match against Naples. The team had not been playing very well in recent matches and no one was putting in too much effort. I was certainly not conscious of putting in any less effort than anybody else. It was a dead game. However, Santos, our coach, was unusually noisy. He kept jumping up and down on the bench and seemed to be having a go at me in particular. He was getting the needle more and more as the game went on until eventually I went to collect the ball from near the dug-out for a throw-in. Santos said something to the referee and the next thing I knew, to my amazement, I was being ordered off the pitch. Santos, my own coach, had sent me off because, he said, I wasn't trying and wasn't obeying his instructions. Little did I realise as I came off the field so ignominiously that I would never again play for Torino.

I never really did fathom out what lay behind that incident although there were several popular theories at the time. One was that the club were angered by my transfer request and wanted to punish me by preventing me from playing for Scotland, which they certainly did.

Another theory was that they wanted to discredit me in front of the fans so that they could sell me and buy Del Sol from Real Madrid in my place. Whichever it was, it wasn't like Santos to behave the way he did. I had always found him to be a very likeable fellow whose weakness probably was that he wasn't tough enough. There is little doubt in my mind that, for whatever reason, Santos was acting under instructions.

After the match, which Naples won 2–0, both goals being scored after my departure, the Torino president, Angelo Filippone, said to the press: 'This means that Law will not be released for Scotland's match against Uruguay on 2 May. We got the impression Law was holding himself back for that game.' He then confirmed that Manchester United had made an approach for me but said, 'We have no intention of selling Law, despite what happened this afternoon. We will discipline him, but he stays with us. We are also keeping Baker'. I was suspended for a fortnight and told not to go anywhere near the ground. Looking back on it now I can honestly say that I was not deliberately saving myself for the match against Uruguay. Like the rest of the team I was not taking the cup tie too seriously, so I suppose there was some justification in what they said. But if I was guilty of 'not trying', then so were the rest of the team.

I started my suspension still not realising that I would never kick another ball for Torino. The team had gone up to Lausanne in Switzerland to play a match in the Friendship Cup competition, when I got a message to make my way up there by train.

Travelling by rail in a foreign country can be a bit of an ordeal, especially when you don't speak the language and have to change trains, but I travelled cheerfully because I had been told that I was on my way to meet Messrs Busby, Edwards, and Hardman of Manchester United to talk about a transfer. The United manager and directors had already been dragged all over Europe by Torino in an attempt to clinch my transfer, and at one point Matt Busby had become so disgusted by the way the Italian club had messed them about that he had said he was no longer interested in the deal. Now, happily, it seemed that at last the difficulties had been overcome. United were touring in Europe and Gigi and I were to meet Matt and the two United directors in a Lausanne night club.

When we got there I was told that Torino had agreed to release me and it was simply a matter of whether or not I wanted to join United. It took me less than three seconds to say yes, and the details of the deal were settled between us there and then. The following day the United party went to rejoin their team and I returned to Turin to pack my bag. I was still being treated like an outcast by Torino, and I was made to travel alone, but that didn't matter. I was going home; or at least I thought I was.

That meeting in Lausanne was the conclusion of a chain of events I had set in motion myself some weeks earlier. From the moment I had decided that I was determined to get out of Italian football, there was really only one team on my mind: Manchester United. After all, Matt Busby had been a recurring figure in my career; hadn't he offered Huddersfield Town £10,000 for my services when I was only 16, and unknown? Wasn't he the man who had given me my first Scotland cap at the age of 18? Hadn't he said that he would have bid for me two years earlier, when I left Huddersfield, but for being particularly well served at inside-forward at that time? Well now things had changed, United were going through a bad spell, and there clearly was room for new faces at Old Trafford.

As early as November 1961, when I had been in Italy only a matter of weeks, I played for the Italian League team against the Football League, at Old Trafford. I was already disillusioned by the Italian scene, even then, and when I met Matt Busby at the banquet after the match and he asked me how I was getting on, I told him the truth: that things were not working out as well as I had expected and that I was pretty fed up. There was nothing that either of us could do about it at that time and nothing was said, but being the shrewd man he is I'd be surprised if the idea that I might wind up playing for United didn't cross his mind. I hadn't yet reached the stage though where I was desperate to get away, and of course there was no way that United could make an approach to me in the circumstances which existed. I was under contract to another club. Less than six months later the position had changed completely. Now I had reached the end of my tether. I had made it clear to Torino that I was unhappy and wanted to get out of the second year of my contract so that I could return home.

At the beginning of April, I was released to play for Scotland in the match against England at Hampden Park. There were only a few weeks of the season left and it was important for me to do something quickly if I was to achieve my aim of being back in English football by the start of the following season. I knew that I would not have another chance to see Matt Busby before the end of the season, so I contacted a friend who told me that Matt would be at Hampden for the international, and that he was staying at the Caledonian Hotel in Edinburgh. Through the friend, I arranged to meet Matt at the hotel on the Sunday morning after the match. I'm sure he couldn't have been in much doubt about why I wanted to see him, but I soon made my purpose clear. I told him that I had had it with Italy and was determined to get back to English football. What I wanted to know was whether United would be interested, if I could persuade Torino to release me.

I never had much doubt about what his answer would be, but I was nevertheless delighted when he said that if Denis Law was available for transfer, then Manchester United would definitely be in the bidding. That was all I needed to know. There were still the formalities to be gone through of course, but to all intents and purposes my future as a Manchester United player was set up at that Sunday morning meeting in Edinburgh. I returned to Italy with one aim; to get out of the second year of my contract with Torino.

Having returned to Turin from Lausanne, I was expecting to be called to the club to start completing the papers for my transfer to United. When a club car came to collect me from the apartment the day after my return, I expected to be taken to Torino's headquarters. I was surprised to find that instead I was driven to Juventus's offices where I was greeted by the Torino president, Angelo Filippone, and Umberto Agnelli, the president of Juventus. I was even more surprised when I was informed that Torino had sold my contract to Juventus and all that was required for the deal to be completed was for me to sign the forms which were laid out on Signor Agnelli's desk. I was not simply surprised, I was absolutely astounded!

I had become accustomed to strange happenings in this lunatic country, but this latest development left me speechless. Two days earlier Torino had struck a deal worth £115,000 transferring me to Manchester United. Now, without reference to either me or United, they had 'sold' me to Juventus for £160,000.

When I got my breath back I said, 'I'm sorry, but no way am I signing for Juventus. I'm going back to England to play for Manchester United'.

The bluff having failed, the two presidents then tried very hard to *persuade* me to sign the transfer forms. I was offered a signing-on fee of £12,000 and a contract which would have made me a very wealthy player indeed. At one point Agnelli gave me a gold watch and a gold tie pin. I said, 'There's no point in giving me those, because I'm not staying'. He replied, 'You can take them anyway, they're just gifts'.

It took me a long time to convince the pair of them that despite all the money that was being offered, and despite the fact that Juventus were the top team in Italy, and despite the attraction of playing along-side Charles and Sivori, I had no intention of signing for Juventus. It's purely academic, but had I switched from Torino to Juventus, with rivalry the way it was, I wouldn't have had a friend left in Turin. The persuasion having failed, the bribes turned to threats. In Italian foot-ball it was perfectly legal for a player's contract to be sold from one club to another. I had no say in the matter. If I refused to play for Juventus then they would see to it that I didn't play for anybody. I remember thinking that countries like South Africa and Australia were not then affiliated to FIFA so at least I could go there, but what I was really gambling on was that Torino wouldn't be prepared to sacrifice £115,000 just to stop me from playing.

As soon as I got out of Agnelli's office I went straight back to the apartment. I had one aim in mind – to get out of Italy without further delay. I threw a few things into a bag and rang for a taxi. I telephoned Turin airport and discovered that the only flight to London that day left Milan, eighty miles away, in a few hours time. Joe was still at the ground training, so I scribbled a note to him explaining what had happened, then I took the cab to Milan. Friends at the airport fixed me a seat on the flight, and a few hours later I was in London organising a connection to Aberdeen. I came away from Italy in such a hurry that I left almost all of my personal belongings behind. That didn't matter. No power on earth would get me back to Turin until the question of my future had been sorted out.

When they learned that I had gone, Torino were furious. They sent me a cable demanding that I return to Turin at once. They could send me a dozen cables, I wasn't going back. My ace in the hole was that £115,000. I was banking on that. As I sweated it out in Aberdeen, I had time to reflect on my season in Italy. Torino hadn't done too badly out of me. I was the team's leading goalscorer, with a modest ten goals in twenty-seven league matches. That figure was better than it sounded when you realise that fourteen goals would have made me the leading goalscorer in the Italian League. Joe Baker was our joint second highest scorer, with seven goals but, because of the accident, he had played in only nineteen league matches. Between us we had done a reasonable job, all things considered, and the Club had finished a respectable seventh in the League table. I spent about two months thinking on these things and waiting for news. Then, as my thoughts were reluctantly turning to the prospect of a new career in Australia, I received a telephone call from Jim Rodgers of the Scottish *Daily Record*. Word had just come through from Italy that Torino had given in. Gigi Peronace was on his way to England to complete my transfer to Manchester United. I was to meet him in Manchester.

CHAPTER 5

Settling Down

I signed for Manchester United on 12 July 1962. The fee of £115,000 was a new British record. It was the third time in just over two years that I had been involved in a record-breaking transfer deal, so United were my fourth club in that period. Despite that fact, perhaps even because of it, I had no doubt when I went to Old Trafford that I was going there to stay.

From the moment that I arrived, the idea of moving to another club never entered my head; although, of course, I was once put on the transfer list by Matt Busby, and I did spend my last year in football with Manchester City. United had paid an enormous fee to bring me to Old Trafford and I felt that I had a responsibility to them. I had done my share of wandering and I was ready to settle down. Even had I not been, with the sort of price tag which was now attached to my head, there were few British clubs who could have afforded me – even assuming any had wanted me – and after my experience in Italy there was no way that I would consider playing for a foreign team ever again. I was grateful to be back in English football, where I intended to stay.

Although Matt Busby had already built two great teams at Old Trafford, United were still not as big a name in world football in 1962 as they are today. Playing in Europe and eventually winning the European Cup had a lot to do with building their enormous reputation, coupled with the massive publicity which successful teams have enjoyed since the mid-sixties through the medium of television. Our average attendance at Old Trafford in my first season, for instance, was just over 40,000, compared to the peak figure of 57,759 in our European Cup-winning season five years later. They were certainly a very big club when I went there, but the best in terms of building a reputation was still to come.

Apart from my delight at being back in English football, arriving at Old Trafford had no special excitement for me. After all, I was now a well-travelled man of the world in a footballing sense, and Old Trafford seemed little different from Turin or Maine Road.

Actually, United were not doing particularly well at the time; they had just finished fifteenth in the League, so I was not joining a club riding at the top. They were still in the processs of rebuilding after Munich, but I could see that the potential was there. Matt Busby had a little more money to spend, and I felt that if anyone could build another successful team, it would be him.

I have often been asked what made Matt Busby so special and really it was the simplest thing in the world. He treated his players like human beings! I had been impressed by the way he dealt with players when he had given me my first Scotland cap, and I played in his team at Hampden Park. He was exactly the same at Old Trafford. Apart from Bill Shankly, I had not met anyone else like him in the game. Elsewhere, players were simply numbers and judged solely on what they did on the field. Personal problems were never taken into account. Busby seemed to care about your life off the field, as well as how you performed on it. Were your digs all right? Your family? Your wife? Your children? It got through to me that here was a man who took a great deal of interest in his players' private lives. It made players run through brick walls for him because they knew that he had their interests at heart. The longer you knew him, the more you felt for him, which was why he had everybody doing the things they did.

The impression a lot of people had of him as the benign uncle was not accurate. He could be very tough: firm but fair. He was a keen disciplinarian. Lateness for training, for instance, was severely punished by fines. He was also tough on behaviour, and dress, and always insisted on collar and tie when we were travelling, even in the warmest weather. This was very different from my other clubs where casual dress had been allowed; but I think he was right. The team are the ambassadors of the club and should look smart. I was interested to see that Brian Clough adopted the same policy with his teams.

As for his approach to the game itself, before a match Matt Busby would give a fairly detailed team talk in which he analysed the strengths and weaknesses of opposition players. I hated these sessions because I didn't want to know about the fellow I was playing against, I preferred to get out on to the field and find out for myself.

Sometimes we would have the team talk on a Friday, sometimes on a Saturday, depending on where we were playing. I preferred to have it on Friday because by the time Saturday came along the talk had completely left my mind. I listened to instructions about my role in the game of course, but that was all I was really interested in. In my early days with United I was given a fairly free hand to roam about the field, which is what I loved to do. I liked to be involved in the game. But as the season wore on, we had an acute problem scoring goals. Apart from David Herd and myself, there was no one to score them, and I was detailed to stay up front which sometimes meant not touching the ball for twenty minutes. That didn't please me at all – in fact I hated it, but I realised that it had to be done.

I've always believed that successful football management is a two-man job. Most of the outstanding managers in recent years have had a strong and dependable assistant helping to run the team, even though, in some cases, the number two kept very much in the background publicly. Currently, Brian Clough and Peter Taylor spring to mind, but looking back there have been other great partnerships, such as Mercer and Allison, Shankly and Paisley, and so on.

Matt Busby had an extremely good assistant in Jimmy Murphy. Jimmy had tremendous experience, including a spell handling the Welsh national team. He played a very significant part in making United a successful side. In 1958, while Matt Busby was lying in a Munich hospital fighting for his life, Jimmy temporarily took over the role of manager. His playing staff at that time consisted of two or three survivors from the air-crash, a handful of reserves, and a couple of players hastily signed or borrowed from other clubs. Yet he managed to take them from the fifth round of the FA Cup all the way to the final at Wembley, where they were beaten 2–1 by Bolton Wanderers.

I was still with Huddersfield Town at the time, but I remember travelling over the Pennines to Manchester on Wednesday, 19 February, to watch a makeshift United team take on Sheffield Wednesday in the fifth round tie which had been postponed because of Munich. It was just thirteen days after the crash, and United's first match since the tragedy. I stood in the crowd at the scoreboard end and I'll never forget that fantastic atmosphere. It was something you had to witness to understand. Everyone in the ground seemed to be willing United to win, which they did, 3–0, with a goal from Webster and two from Shay Brennan, who was playing outside-left. Albert Quixall was still a member of the Sheffield Wednesday side, who didn't know what had hit them.

Knowing Jimmy Murphy as I do, I have no doubt that he would have capitalised on the emotional atmosphere to get the very best possible effort out of his players. He was a superb motivator, full of enthusiasm and positive aggression. Because Busby was not really fully fit after Munich, our training was mostly in the hands of Jimmy Murphy. He wanted plenty of grit, and he didn't like cheats; players who thought they had done enough. Everybody's job was to help everybody else in the team. He instilled that into the youth and reserve teams, which over the years brought many great players into the side.

He was a lot like Bill Shankly, except that he was more fearsome: a fierce competitor. Even though he was in his fifties, he loved to take part in five-a-side games. If he got a knock from one of the young players, the lad wouldn't get a volley. Jimmy would say, 'that's what I want, have no respect for me at all'. Sometimes, if Busby was away scouting, Jimmy would give the team talk and it would be a bit different from Matt's, with the emphasis more on letting the opposition know you were there. We sometimes played better for Jimmy than we did for Matt. He was very popular.

His name was often linked with managers' jobs at other clubs, and there's no doubt he could easily have had one had he wanted, but he preferred to remain at Old Trafford as part of the 'team'. It is possibly an over-simplification to say this, but I always felt that while Matt Busby gave United their subtlety and sophistication, it was Jimmy Murphy who put a little bite into our play. Together they were a great combination; a real team effort, which is exactly what football is all about.

One thing I was particularly grateful for at Old Trafford was the way in which all players were treated alike. I was no different from anyone else, which was great. In Italy, and to some extent at Maine Road, I had been treated as the star player, one of the élite. That's fine for a while, but then you begin to realise that everything depends on you and it's a great burden to carry. At Old Trafford everybody was equal. You had a job to do on the field, and you were judged on that. If you did badly, then maybe there was a reason, or maybe you just couldn't play, but it would be sorted out with reason and common sense and a little dignity.

My first season at Old Trafford was an eventful one in which we were very nearly relegated, but went on to win the FA Cup, showing on the one hand that we had problems, but on the other that there really was some potential. After only a few games I could see that we had a much more promising outlook than the one I had experienced at Maine Road, two seasons earlier. Like City, we were faced with an uphill struggle, but at least we had a nucleus of good players, many of them still young. Apart from Bobby Charlton, Albert Quixall and Bill Foulkes with England experience, there was David Herd, like myself a Scottish international; Maurice Setters, an England Under 23 player; Harry Gregg, the Northern Ireland goalkeeper; and three Eire internationals, Tony Dunne, Noel Cantwell, and Johnny Giles. We had a couple of promising youngsters in Phil Chisnall and Mark Pearson; and still to gain international honours but very much on the fringe of them were Shay Brennan and Nobby Stiles. I felt a bit sorry for these two, both of whom played in more than thirty league matches that season. They were both utility men, playing in three or four different positions during the season. Neither had yet established himself in a regular berth in the team, and both missed the FA Cup Final after playing in four of the earlier rounds. Nobby lost his place for both the semi-final and the final to Pat Crerand, who had been cup-tied in the early rounds. Nobby was in the awful position of being out of the side for league matches, but stepping in, in place of Pat, for the cup-ties. Another man who missed the Cup Final was Harry Gregg. Harry was a great goalkeeper, but he was unfortunately plagued by injury, and seemed to be out of the side almost as often as he was in it. It didn't help the team's stability to have so much uncertainty in such a vital position.

Bobby Charlton had undergone a hernia operation during the summer, so he was missing from the team when we met West Bromwich Albion at Old Trafford on the opening day of the 1962–63 season. It was a glorious summery afternoon but I was feeling just a little apprehensive, knowing that with my massive transfer tag the spectators would be expecting something special from me. I desperately wanted to do well, and things could hardly have gone better. David Herd shot us into the lead after only five minutes, then two minutes later Johnny Giles sent over a cross from the right which I managed to head into the net. The match was only seven minutes old, yet we were leading 2–0 and I had scored a goal on my debut. Unfortunately, that was not the end of the story – West Brom fought back to earn a two-all draw, but at least I had made a reasonable start with my new club.

In a way, that match against West Brom set the tone for the season and highlighted some of our problems. We could create and score goals, but as a team we were not strong enough and opponents often found it too easy to score goals against us. British football had not yet become afflicted by defensive tactics. The game was still about scoring more goals than the other side. That was the great success of the Spurs side: they went out with the attitude 'if they score two, we'll score three'. We tried to adopt the same approach at Old Trafford, but unfortunately we had the ratio wrong. Too often our opponents scored more than we did. This was never better illustrated than when we met Leicester City in a league match at Filbert Street at Easter. I scored a hat-trick in that match and yet we still lost 4–3. To put the result into true perspective it should be added that Leicester were enjoying very nearly the best season in their history at the time. They were fancied to win the championship, and at one time were hoping to pull off the league and FA Cup double. In the end they won neither.

Playing the way we did, we were involved in a number of high-scoring matches. One of our best early season results was a 3–1 win over Arsenal at Highbury, when a member of the Arsenal line-up was my old mate Joe Baker who had escaped from Italy a few weeks after me. In November, we beat the reigning champions, Ipswich, 5–3 at Portman Road. I scored four goals in that match, then scored four more four days later in Scotland's 5–1 win over Northern Ireland at Hampden Park. After my experience of tight marking in Italy, I was finding it far easier to score goals in British football, because there was so much more time and space available. The marking was exactly the same as it had been before I left, and I found that I could lose players far more easily than I could before I went to Italy. In league matches alone I scored twenty-three goals in my first season back, thirty more in my second season, and twenty-eight in my third. That was a total of eighty-one goals in a hundred and four league matches. Although I had found the *life* in Italy unacceptable, there is no doubt that the *experience* made me a better player.

The same thing seems to have worked for Kevin Keegan, who has clearly become a better player for England after a spell in the German league, where they also employ man-marking tactics. In his first twenty-odd games for England – before he went to Germany – Kevin did nothing out of the ordinary. His contribution was often negligible. But after a season with Hamburg he was transformed. He was voted European Footballer of the Year in 1978, largely on the strength of some superb performances for England, and there is no doubt in my mind that playing in Germany has made him a better player; just as it did for me playing in Italy. It may not work for everybody, but if you have the basic ability and the determination to succeed, then the keener competition brings it out.

No one appreciated the value of broadening football horizons more than Matt Busby. He had been Britain's principal European pioneer, and although due to circumstances United no longer qualified for any of the major European competitions, he maintained the club's contact with Europe by arranging friendly matches against the very best European teams. Since Munich, United had struck up a great friendship with the Spanish giants, Real Madrid. The two teams had met regularly over the previous three seasons, and on 13 December 1961 United had the satisfaction of beating the team which had won the European Cup five years in succession, for the first time in six attempts with a 3–1 victory at Old Trafford. I was not with United at that time, of course, but on 19 September 1962 I was in the United side which became the first British team to beat Real in their own magnificent Bernabeu Stadium, when we won 2–0. Six days later we met the only other side to have won the European Cup, the reigning champions, Benfica, at Old Trafford, and achieved a very satisfactory 2–2 draw.

Although we could achieve such encouraging results in friendly matches against Europe's footballing aristocrats, on the domestic front our results were erratic and throughout the 1962–63 season, we were always too close to the relegation zone. We had the basis of a decent side, but we still lacked somebody on the wing, and in particular we were weak in midfield where various permutations from Nobby Lawton, Nobby Stiles, Jimmy Nicholson and Maurice Setters were doing a competent job, but one which wasn't good enough for a team which had its sights set on winning championships.

Maurice became a good friend of mine. He and Noel Cantwell, and later Pat Crerand, and I usually found ourselves together whenever the team travelled. Maurice had the reputation of being a hard man, but that wasn't really true. He was a very enthusiastic player who never stopped chasing. He made up for his lack of real ability by getting stuck in, but no way was he a dirty player as some people said. He had a pretty rugged physique, and he also had a crewcut, which gave him rather a fearsome look. I suppose therefore his appearance, coupled with his tremendous enthusiasm, made him look a much harder player than he actually was. Off the field he was as soft as putty.

Wing-half was our most serious problem, which wasn't properly sorted out until the following season, when we had Pat Crerand at right-half, with Nobby Stiles playing a dual role of left-half and sweeper. But we also had a serious problem on the wing, and I could never understand why we didn't use Bobby Charlton more in that position. For me, that was his best position. I've always felt that he was wasted in midfield, even though I know he spent most of his career playing there. It may sound a little ridiculous to say that Matt Busby and Alf Ramsey were both wrong, in view of the success that each of them had in winning the European and World Cups, with Bobby in the midfield role, but I do believe that they were successful in spite of the fact rather than because of it. To me, Bobby Charlton was one of the finest wingers in the world. Playing in midfield he would invariably hit long raking passes out to the flanks, which was fine from the spectator point of view because it looked spectacular. But it was also terrific for the opposition because it gave defenders time to reorganise. Whenever Scotland met England we were happy to see Bobby in midfield – he wouldn't cause us problems from there, but put him on the wing and that was a different story. He had phenomenal speed which could take him past any full-back. He could get to the bye-line and either chip balls back or across with that magical left foot, and cause all sorts of problems. I've always believed that United would have scored far more goals if Bobby had been used more in this way. I could never understand why he wasn't.

Ironically, the one man who did play consistently on our right-wing, including the FA Cup Final, was Johnny Giles, who later became regarded as one of the great midfield players of his generation. With Matt Busby's vision and successful record in the transfer market, people often ask how he came to let Giles go to Leeds for £35,000, which even in 1963 wasn't a particularly large sum of money. The simple fact is that Giles was not an outstanding player at Old Trafford. He was a very ordinary winger, and not a particularly brave one. He had done nothing to show where his real potential lay up to the time he left. It was Don Revie who discovered his talent as a midfield player. Perhaps if Giles had stayed at Old Trafford longer, Matt Busby might have made the same discovery, but I suppose you can't win them all and from Matt's point of view that was one that he lost. As it happened, it didn't matter too much anyway, because by the time Giles left, United already had Pat Crerand doing exactly the same sort of job which Giles later did for Leeds.

If joining Manchester United had been the start of my settling down period, then I suppose the process was completed on Tuesday, 11 December 1962, when I married Diana Rosemary Leith Thomson. Di and I had met during the summer of that year at, of all places, the local dance hall in Aberdeen, where she was a secretary in a solicitor's office. Our courtship was a brief one, carried on by courtesy of British European Airways. When the football season began, I flew home to see her every Saturday night after the match. Wherever we were playing I sorted out the flight timetables to find the quickest way to Aberdeen. I had Matt Busby's full approval to do this. He liked his players to be married because he believed that it helped stabilize their lives. He felt that it was good to have a family to go home to, someone to care for, a bit of responsibility. It was better than gallivanting about the town – a steadying influence. When you were treated like god at Old Trafford, it would be easy to stay up in the clouds. Coming home to nappies and dirty dishes brings you back to earth pretty quickly.

Di and I eventually had five children – Gary, Andrew, Robert, Iain and Diana – innings closed. But we had a pretty hard time in the first few months of wedlock. A fortnight after we were married the country was gripped by one of the worst freeze-ups in living memory. It was so bad that the football league programme was brought to a complete standstill for seven weeks. It was during that period that the pools panel first came into being. Everything was frozen. We newly-weds had just moved into a club house in Chorlton-cum-Hardy, and our living conditions were, to say the least, spartan. We had no carpets on the floor – just bare boards. We had a bed, a television, a couple of armchairs and a cooker, and that was about it. There was no central heating; we were absolutely freezing. It was a pretty harrowing time for both of us. We had known one another for six months and Di was living away from home for the first time in her life. She had left the warmth of a comfortable home in Aberdeen to live in this refrigerated tomb with me. I couldn't help making the mental comparison between our present dilemma and the warmth and luxury of the apartment from which I had fled in Italy; not to mention the warm and comfortable digs I had left just a mile or so away where Mr and Mrs Atkins had looked after me like one of their own family. It was a hard introduction to married life, but we came through it all right and were probably better for having done so.

Di was never much of a football fan, which was fine because I always tried to keep my private and professional lives separate. The only football match she watched that season was the FA Cup Final at Wembley, when of course all the players' wives and girlfriends were there. I never did much talking to the press, or on television, while I was playing football. I always insisted that anyone who did want to talk to me about football did so at the ground. Those who did find their way to my front door – and there were one or two that did – were politely but firmly turned away.

Not even weddings interrupt the pattern of a football season, and four days after I was married I was back at 'work' playing in a league match at West Bromwich, where I was to make one of the biggest mistakes of my life.

The referee was a man named Gilbert Pullin, whom I didn't know from Adam but who seemed to spend the entire match making abusive remarks to me. If I had a shot at goal and the ball went wide, there would be this little referee at my side saying 'Oh you clever so and so, you can't play'. I was flabbergasted and at half-time I mentioned what was happening to Matt Busby. He told me to try and put it out of my mind and get on with the game. Had the comments stopped then, I'm sure that that would have been the end of the affair. But they didn't stop. The needling went on throughout the second half, and genuinely put me off my game.

After the match, which we lost 3–0, I had another talk with Matt Busby and we decided that we had no alternative but to report the matter to the FA – which turned out to be the worst thing I could have done. We were called to a meeting in London where a disciplinary committee listened to all the evidence, then decided that Mr Pullin should be severely censured. Mr Pullin was unhappy about the verdict and decided to quit. His career as a referee came to an end with that hearing. Although there is no doubt that he was completely in the wrong in what he did, I felt sorry for him when I realised what the

Denis Law

consequences were. What I did not realise at the time was the effect that these events would have on my own career.

It did not occur to me until years later, but there is no doubt in my mind now that from that moment on, in the minds of some referees, I was a marked man. That is the only possible explanation I can think of for some of the victimisation that I suffered over the next few seasons. I do not claim to have been a saint, and there is no doubt that there were many occasions when I got myself into trouble, but there were numerous other occasions when I felt that I was being picked on by overzealous officials. If I was involved in a skirmish with another player, hardly ever was I given the benefit of the doubt. Over the next three seasons I was sent off three times and received staggeringly heavy punishments, when in each of the three cases I was the victim of extreme provocation. In each case I retaliated, but looking back on those years I can only conclude now that, in some cases, *I* was the victim of retaliation.

A significant date in the 1962–63 season was 6 February 1963: the fifth anniversary of Munich, and also the day that Paddy Crerand joined us from Celtic. I'm happy to say that I was instrumental in bringing Paddy to Old Trafford. Before he made the signing, Matt Busby confided to me that he was considering signing a wing-half, which as I've already said was a position we desperately needed to fill. The choice was between Pat Crerand of Celtic and Jim Baxter of Rangers. Which did I think we should go for?

Matt fancied them both. I said that there was no doubt about who was the better player. That was Jimmy Baxter. But I doubted whether he would be able to turn it on consistently in the hurly-burly of the English first division. If we wanted somebody who would be more reliable over a longer period, then the man to choose was Pat Crerand. The choice was made, and Pat joined us to become a vital piece in the jigsaw of the third great team which Matt Busby was building.

Pat Crerand was the only player I knew at the time who could be both brilliant and pathetic in the same game, which was a great asset. I've seen many good players play badly and drift right out of a game. Pat didn't. If he was having a bad game he would persevere and play himself through it. Steve Coppell is a bit like that. Pat would just carry on until something did go right, and then he would start to spray around those beautiful passes which were his hallmark. He hit some magnificent balls. He was always looking to hit balls over defenders or inside the full-back, or inside the centre-half. He was similar to Johnny Haynes, although I thought Pat was more direct. Like Bobby Charlton, Haynes played a lot of balls to the wing. Pat was always looking for that direct diagonal ball which was the killer. People said that he

68

played to me a lot, but that wasn't really true. His passes did often come to me, but that was because I was always there looking to make the run, rather than because he was looking for me.

Pat's distribution was immaculate, and he also had the asset of being a great reader of the game. He read it in a positive way, spotting where he could make a telling interception that would turn defence into attack. He cut out a tremendous number of balls through his intelligent reading of situations. He always wanted the ball too, which was another great quality; a bit like John White of Spurs. If you were in difficulties there would always be a call from Pat. I loved playing with him. He and I made some terrific runs down the flank, just knocking the ball to one another.

Pat Crerand was the master of delicate chips and flicks. People would think 'Where on earth is that going?'; then suddenly I would be on the end of it, or later on Besty. The big weakness in Pat's game, which he hated to admit, was that he couldn't defend. The following season, when Nobby Stiles had established his role in the side, part of his job was to cover for Pat. Pat was always liable to be caught out hitting a ball square, and if he was beaten he couldn't recover because he hadn't the speed. I used to say that he was a great asset to television because they didn't need slow motion when he was on the ball. That was his weakness, but it was more than made up for by his massive positive contribution to the game.

Pat joined us just a couple of weeks before the resumption of football following the freeze-up. Because of it the season had needed to be extended and the Cup Final was put back three weeks until the end of May. We didn't play our third round match against my old club, Huddersfield Town, until 4 March; then we played three rounds in the space of thirteen days. We had the good fortune to be drawn at home in all three rounds, and after beating Huddersfield 5–0, a match in which I scored a hat-trick, we beat Aston Villa 1–0, and then Chelsea 2–1.

A fortnight later we had our first away match in the competition and beat second division Coventry 3–1. In the semi-final draw, we had another piece of luck when instead of meeting either Liverpool or Leicester City, we were paired with second division Southampton.

I've always believed that the semi-final is the worst round of any cup competition, because of what is at stake. This match turned out to be one of the scrappiest I ever played in, which seemed to prove my point. Even the single goal by which we won was a sloppy affair, although some people said at the time that it showed the versatility of Denis Law. What actually happened was that I took a swing at the ball and didn't connect properly, but as I fell on the floor the ball got caught under my leg. I was lying on my back in the goal-mouth when I managed to get a second stab at it and scoop it out of Ron Reynolds reach into the corner of the net.

In the dying minutes of the game Southampton almost equalised when David Gaskell was caught off his line and lobbed, but he just managed to get a hand to it and turned it over the bar. It seemed that the fates had decreed that we should go to Wembley, although the same fates had apparently also decided that, before we did, there would be one almighty scramble to retain our first division status.

After spending most of the season at the wrong end of the league table we came to face our last four matches knowing that either we, Birmingham City or Manchester City would be joining Leyton Orient, who were already certain to make the drop. As so often happens in those situations, three of our last four fixtures were against those very three teams. We went to St Andrews and lost 2–1 to Birmingham, which meant that our next game against Manchester City at Maine Road would be virtually a relegation 'derby'.

One of the Manchester clubs was now almost certain to go down, and the outcome of this match would probably determine which. City were in slightly worse shape than we were. They desperately needed both points whereas, for us, a draw would be a good result. Alex Harley gave City the lead early in the game and they looked like holding on to it until their goalkeeper, Harry Dowd, inexplicably dragged me to the ground in the second half. I was inside the penalty area chasing a diagonal through ball, which I had little hope of catching, when Harry caught me in a rugby tackle and United were awarded a penalty.

I couldn't watch the kick being taken, but little Albert Quixall kept a cool head and slotted it home to give us a very fortunate point, which almost certainly consigned City to the second division. We now needed just one more point from our two remaining fixtures, while City had to win their last match of the season, away to West Ham, to have any chance of survival. Things looked black for us for a while when Leyton Orient scored the first goal in our match at Old Trafford, but we overcame the setback and eventually won 3–1. City, meanwhile, were getting hammered 6–1 at Upton Park and went down. Our struggle had gone on right up to the last Saturday of the league season. Seven days later we would be at Wembley for the Cup Final.

We still had one outstanding league fixture, away to Nottingham Forest, which was played on the Monday evening of Wembley week. I was one of several players rested from a meaningless match which we lost 3–2. That result was hardly surprising since by now, with relegation avoided, there was only one subject on the minds of everyone at

Old Trafford. We had had our share of luck in getting to the Cup Final, but there was nothing lucky about our performance on the day. In a strange way, I believe that our fight to avoid relegation helped us to win the Cup. It had kept us on our toes right to the end of the season. We were all keyed up, but with the threat of relegation out of the way, now we could relax and get down to playing football.

Leicester, on the other hand, had had the disappointment of seeing their championship challenge fail and I feel sure that for them the process was working in reverse. They had been faced with five of their last six league matches away from home, and as they had dropped points and seen their championship hopes fade, so I believe they had mentally run down. Nevertheless they were red hot favourites to win the Cup, which was another good thing for us. It's great to be the underdog at Wembley, because then you have nothing to lose. We were able to go out without pressure and play our natural game.

The 1962–63 season had been a year of building. There were still one or two pieces of the jigsaw missing, but we ended the season a better side than when the season began; a fact which had been largely obscured by our desperate fight for survival. Although I'm sure that none of us realised it at the time, we were now ready to give an indication of our true potential. The FA Cup Final was to be our finest performance of the season. Our team was: Gaskell, Dunne, Cantwell (captain), Crerand, Foulkes, Setters, Giles, Quixall, Herd, Law, Charlton.

Wembley is a great place for a team who can stroke the ball about. If you have skilful players and can get on top and get a bit of time, you can destroy opponents at Wembley. We had the players who could do that. We had little Albert Quixall, who was a good player on the ball – not the greatest fighter in the world, he'd be the first to admit that – but certainly skilful. We had Bobby Charlton and Pat Crerand who could stroke the ball around with the best, and we had big David Herd who, like Bobby, could fire in tremendous shots from all angles. We had a bit of toughness in defence, a combination of the lot really. The football we played that day marked the turning point in our fortunes. Instead of fighting to avoid relegation, the following season we would finish runners-up in the League.

It was a beautiful sunny day on 25 May 1963, and the game was only fifteen minutes old when I took a pass from Pat Crerand and beat Gordon Banks from close range, to score my sixth FA Cup goal of the season. I've always believed that the team who scores first at Wembley is going to win the Cup. It doesn't always work out like that, of course, but when David Herd scored a second before half-time I felt that the Cup was as good as ours. Then Keyworth pulled one back for them, and suddenly there were doubts.

Leicester were a similar side to United in that they relied basically on attacking football. We always seemed to be involved in high scoring matches with them; was this to be another? The fears didn't last long before David Herd had restored our two-goal margin with his second goal of the match, and it was all over. United had ended the season on a high note, and I had won my very first medal in professional football. Year after year I had seen the delight on the faces of the players on the winning side in FA Cup Finals – now I knew how they felt. Somehow, there is nothing quite like winning a cup winner's medal at Wembley. I should have hated to have gone there and lost.

CHAPTER 6

The Highest Honour

Winning the FA Cup brought relief not only to Manchester United, but also to me personally. Three times in succession clubs had paid out record transfer fees for me. Things hadn't worked out with Torino, and both Manchester City and United had almost been relegated with me in the side. Some people were beginning to suggest that the coincidence was too great. Maybe I was a one-man band. Suggestions like that hurt very deeply, and they weren't true. Winning the FA Cup killed that kind of speculation and took away a bit of the pressure. For the first time in my career I was with a club where the future outlook had begun to look rosy. At Wembley there had been clear signs that the team was about to turn the corner. There were still a few improvements to be made, but everyone at the club had the feeling that there were better days ahead. The 1963–64 season was to confirm that feeling.

Unfortunately, our Wembley victory had an unhappy sequel. Having won the Cup, we were expecting to receive a substantial bonus. No actual figure had been discussed, but we knew that the previous season's beaten finalists, Burnley, had been on £1000 a man, and there were reports that Leicester City had been on a similar bonus to beat us. We knew that a bonus was due, and we were expecting something in the region of four figures. That summer we went on a close-season tour of Italy and played our first match in Turin, of all places, against Juventus. We had been in Italy only a few days when Matt Busby announced that our Cup Final bonus was to be £20 per man. Everyone was flabbergasted. Surprise quickly turned to anger and a deputation of players went to see Matt, but it had no effect. His explanation was that Mr Hardman, the club chairman, had felt embarrassed about having to ask the Board for money for winning the Cup after we had done so badly throughout the season in the League. That was the position, and although we were far from happy about it, we had to accept it. We were all so embarrassed about the size of the bonus that, although there had been speculation in the newspapers that we were to get around £2000 a man, no one to my knowledge said anything about it outside the club until years later.

Today, of course, bonuses are agreed at the start of the season and form part of a player's contract. In 1963, the game was still going through a financial transition. The maximum wage had not long been abolished, and bonuses for winning trophies were an innovation. It didn't take us long to learn our lesson. The season following our Cup Final win, we met Sporting Club of Lisbon in the quarter-final of the European Cup-Winners' Cup. After we had won the first leg, 4–1 at Old Trafford, it was announced that we were on £500 a man to win the trophy. Ironically, when we went to Lisbon for the return leg we were thrashed 5–0. Our bonus went down the drain, but at least an important new principle had been established. Never again would we be offered a derisory £20 for winning a major trophy.

Although we were brought sharply down to earth following our Cup Final victory when the league champions, Everton, beat us 4–0 in the Charity Shield, we started the 1963–64 season in cracking style. We had revenge over Everton with a 5–1 win at Old Trafford, in our third match of the season; then we went to Portman Road and thrashed Ipswich 7–2. After seven matches we were top of the league with twelve points from a possible fourteen. It was the second season in succession that we had thrashed Ipswich in front of their own supporters. The previous year I had scored four goals in our 5–3 victory. This time, I had three out of our seven. I was still finding the net with great regularity, and this was to be my best season for scoring goals. Apart from thirty in thirty league matches, I also hit nine in six FA Cup ties, and six more in five European matches. During the summer I had scored a hat-trick when Scotland were beaten 4–3 by Norway in Bergen. In November we beat them 6–1 at Hampden Park, and this time I scored four.

The summer had also brought me a new honour for Scotland. Our captain, Dave Mackay, was injured during the match in Bergen and was unfit to play in our remaining tour matches against the Republic of Ireland and Spain. I was made captain for both games. We lost the first, 1–0, in Dublin, but beat Spain 6–2, in Madrid, when I again managed to get on to the scoresheet.

I suppose my reputation as a goalscorer must have played a large part in helping me to win the greatest honour of my career. That came on 23 October 1963, when I was selected to represent the Rest of the World against England, at Wembley, in a match to mark the centenary of the FA. It was an experience beyond my wildest dreams to be chosen to line up with such legendary figures. Of the world's great players, only Pele, who was injured, was missing. There was the captain of the Brazilian World Cup-winning side, Djalma Santos; Alfredo Di

Stefano, who had won five successive European Cup Winners' Medals as a member of the brilliant Real Madrid side; Ferenc Puskas, whom I could remember playing for the great Hungarian side which had destroyed England at Wembley ten years earlier, when I was only a boy; Yashin, Kopa, Masopust; the list seemed endless. We all met up on the Sunday before the game, still not knowing who was going to play in the side.

The tension was terrific. I wanted to play so much, but these people had travelled from all over the world – surely they would all get a game – I had only travelled from Manchester. To be selected to play in such company was the highest honour a player could receive; an honour not only for me I felt, but also for Scotland. Apart from myself, the only other British player involved was my Scotland colleague, Jim Baxter. Sixteen world players took part in the match in which the team that took the field was: Yashin (Russia); D. Santos (Brazil), Schnellinger (West Germany); Pluskal, Popluhar, Masopust (all Czechoslovakia); Kopa (France), Law (Scotland), Di Stefano (Spain); Eusebio (Portugal) and Gento (Spain).

In the second half, Soskic (Yugoslavia), Eyzaguirre (Chile), Baxter (Scotland), Seeler (West Germany) and Puskas (Hungary) came on in the places of Yashin, Santos, Masopust, Kopa and Eusebio.

The match itself was an exhibition, with the Rest team showing off their skills. England took the game far more seriously and won 2–1. Even playing exhibition football, I could feel the tremendous talent of the men around me. Thanks to Puskas, who laid on the pass, I even had the satisfaction of scoring our only goal. He picked up a ball about thirty to forty yards out and started to make a run through the inside-left channel. At the same time, to give him an option, I made a run through the inside-right channel and called for the ball. With his tremendous left foot I imagined he would have a pop at goal himself, but being the great player he was, he saw that I was in a better position and gave me the ball to slip past Gordon Banks from almost exactly the same spot that I had done a few months earlier in the FA Cup Final, for Manchester United. That was the climax to a fantastic day. Nothing I ever did in football gave me more pleasure than playing in that match.

My career seemed to be on the up and up. I was playing for a United side which was among the League leaders, and things had never looked better. It seemed I could scarcely put a foot wrong and I suppose I was inevitably destined for a fall. That came on 16 November 1963, when I was sent off in a league match against Aston Villa at Villa Park.

It was a match we were destined to lose 4–0, even though Villa were among the half dozen teams struggling at the wrong end of the league table. Throughout the game I was having problems with their wing-half, Alan Deakin, who seemed to be kicking me as often as he kicked the ball. Early in the second half he lunged at me once again and ended up sliding between my legs. I was so incensed that as he lay there on the ground, I made an angry gesture as if to strike him with the inside of my thigh. It was no more than a gesture, and I certainly didn't make contact, but the next thing I knew the referee, Mr Jim Carr of Sheffield, was pointing to the dressing room and I was on my way for an early bath.

Apart from the incident with Santos in Italy, that was the first time in my career that I had been sent off. It was an awful feeling leaving the field alone with more than half an hour of the match to play, and what made it particularly hard to swallow was the knowledge that while I was suffering the ultimate penalty, the man who had caused the trouble was being allowed to get on with the game. It always seemed to happen that way, that the man retaliating was sent off while the insti-gator of trouble often went unpunished. Defenders were given the job of marking a key player and then, when the trouble started, it was the forward who got sent off although he was usually the one who was being kicked. Matt Busby used to say 'count to ten'. I never got past five. If a fellow gave me a crack, I lost my temper there and then and I'd want to crack him back. I couldn't switch it on and off like an electric light bulb. Some players could wait half an hour and then take retribu-tion. That to me really was premeditated violence. If I was going to retaliate it came out in the heat of the moment.

Instead of bleating about bad conduct on the field, the game's administrators should have done far more than they did to protect players from rough tackling. People pay their money to watch skilful players performing to the best of their ability, not to see them being hacked down by hired assassins. The FA did of course introduce the restriction on tackling from behind in the early seventies, and that was an improvement for a time, but it was too little and too late. For one thing it was too late to stop Jimmy Greaves hanging up his boots pre-maturely. One of the reasons Jimmy quit the game was because he was sick of being kicked and getting no protection from referees. No sooner had he quit than they brought in this new clamp-down. I remember thinking at the time that Greavesey had packed it in too early.

Having been sent off, I knew that I would not get much leniency from the FA Disciplinary Committee. My disciplinary record was not good. Before I went to Italy I had received a seven-day suspension for accumulated bookings, which I never actually served due to the Italian season starting later than the English one. By November of 1963 I had already collected three cautions during the current season, so I suppose I expected them to throw the book at me, despite the fact that I was something of an innocent party. Even so, I was staggered when I learned that my punishment was to be a twenty-eight day suspension.

Such a savage sentence was something new in the game and it seemed that the FA had introduced a new set of rules for dealing with me personally. Suspension meant a complete loss of income and also, during the period of the ban, I was not allowed to go near the ground. That was ludicrous. I was being deprived of my livelihood and also prevented from keeping in shape to start earning it again once the ban was over. A professional footballer has to keep fit, and to do that he needs the facilities of the club. It's fine going for a run in the park, but to be a professional player you have got to have professional training. I was being robbed of all that, in addition to nearly a thousand pounds in lost wages and bonuses. When I was suspended again, almost exactly a year later, the situation had changed slightly so that, although I lost my income on that occasion, I was allowed to attend training at the ground during the ban. It wasn't until some time later that the PFA managed to force a change which allowed players to be paid part of their salary while they were suspended.

My last match before suspension was on 7 December, against Stoke City at Old Trafford. I wanted to sign off with a flourish, and as luck would have it I did manage to score four goals in our 5–2 victory. A few days before the Stoke match we lost 2–0 to Tottenham Hotspur in the first leg of our European Cup-Winners' Cup tie at White Hart Lane.

Spurs were the outstanding team of that period; they had done the double in 1961, then retained the FA Cup the following year, and won the European Cup-Winners' Cup in 1963. When we met them, they were defending it, as the holders. My suspension meant that I missed the return leg, which United won 4–1, after extra time, in a tremendously exciting match in which Dave Mackay broke his leg. Dave was a marvellous competitor: tough but scrupulously fair. It was his style of play to go for balls where he appeared to have no chance, and yet as often as not he would come out of the tackle with the ball and then produce an excellent pass. On this occasion I was sitting in the stand and I remember Dave and Noel Cantwell going for the ball and thinking to myself, 'Dave, you've no chance'. This time there was a collision and as Dave went down it was obvious what had happened. I came out of the stand just as the St John's ambulance men carried him off the field and I went down to the treatment room with him. He was obviously in a lot of pain and he knew that his leg was broken. Dave wasn't a good colour at the best of times, but then he was as white as a ghost. He was lying on the table soaked in his own sweat and yet he was cold.

Dave Mackay was one of the finest wing-halves in the game. He had a marvellous combination of defensive and attacking qualities. He and Danny Blanchflower were the heart of that magnificent Spurs side which for my money played the best football I've seen any British side play. They had so many outstanding players: Blanchflower was the complete creative genius; in goal they had Scotland's Bill Brown; John White, at inside-forward, was one of the best and most underrated players I've seen in that position; Bobby Smith gave them strength at centre-forward and, for his size, Cliff Jones was one of the best headers of the ball in the game. Then there was strength at full-back, with Baker and Henry, and a solid centre-half in Maurice Norman; Medwin and Dyson provided good alternative possibilities on the wing, and the icing on the cake was Jimmy Greaves.

In my opinion, Jimmy Greaves was the finest striker I ever saw. I would put him ahead of everybody. To be fair, I didn't see much of Pele, and when I did see him in the 1966 World Cup I didn't see him at his best. On what I did see of all the best men in the world, Jimmy Greaves is definitely the top of my list. He could score goals from anywhere out of nothing. They said his work rate was low. Well I've never believed that you should judge a player on work rate. Jimmy Greaves was there to score goals, and he scored plenty. Nobody did it better. He profited a lot from the hard work of John White, but that's what football is all about. It's a team game, and there was no better team than Spurs. They played football as it should be played; everyone playing for everyone else, with goals coming from all positions. They were absolute class. I believe that United eventually became as good a team, and so too, currently, have Liverpool, but no one else, to my way of thinking, ever did.

I didn't see the United sides of 1948 and the middle fifties, so I can't include them in the comparison. The United side I played for had some memorable tussles with that great Spurs side over the years, and our record against them was actually very good. I think that we came out just about on top as far as results go.

Great teams must have great players and by the time I returned to Old Trafford after suspension, a major new factor had been introduced into our team: George Best.

George Best actually made his first appearance for United against West Bromwich Albion at Old Trafford on 14 September 1963. Johnny Giles had been sold to Leeds United and I was injured, which gave George the opportunity to make his debut a couple of months before becoming a regular member of the side. He was still only 17. I sat with Matt Busby during that match and I remember wondering whether or not George would actually make the grade. We knew that he had plenty of skill, but he was so skinny and frail that I was really afraid that he might not be strong enough to survive in first class football. I said to Matt that it would all depend on how much stick he was able to take. One thing in his favour was that playing on the wing, as he did at the time, he wouldn't come into quite so much physical contact as he would in an inside-forward's role.

Whatever my reservations about George's physique, there was no doubting his ability. He was superb. He had everything I liked in a player. He was brave; he never shirked a tackle; he could kick with either foot; he was a great header of the ball, and of course he was tremendously skilful. As it turned out he was also quite strong enough to take care of himself. Having made that single appearance in September, George finally came back into the side on 28 December 1963, while I was still under suspension. Two days earlier, on Boxing Day, United had been thrashed 6–1 by Burnley at Turf Moor. This time they had revenge with a 5–1 win at Old Trafford. George scored his first league goal and from that day forward he was never out of the side except through injury or suspension.

Of course, it is history now that George Best went on to become one of the outstanding and most controversial figures in football. Being the way he was I suppose it is inevitable that people continually want to know what he was like as a team mate. I liked him a great deal and in some ways I felt sorry for him. He certainly had a lot of pressure to live with, although I think he would admit that he created a bit of that himself.

The publicity business started in 1965, after we had beaten Benfica 5–1 in Lisbon and the papers had christened him *El Beatle*. He became the first footballer in Britain to be treated like a film star. I suppose his appearance, and the fact that he was single, made him a natural target for the publicity men. He just looked and acted the part of the superstar. Some of the less able players used to resent it, but it didn't bother me. My attitude was that what a fellow did off the field was his own business. I was only concerned about what he did on it, and there was nothing wrong with George Best from that point of view.

Publicity was one thing, but something few people seemed to realise was that later on George had a great deal of worry over the situation in Northern Ireland. His family were living over there and he was threatened on several occasions. That can't have been easy to live with. He was basically a very lonely figure, even though he was always surrounded by a crowd. Most of them were hangers-on. It may sound corny, but I've always believed that the thing George really needed was a wife. Somehow, though, he just couldn't seem to manage it. He had this magnificent house built at Bramhall, but he had no one really to share it with him. I've often wondered how different he might have been had he been able to settle down. Matt Busby did everything he could to help. On one occasion he even asked George to live at his home as a member of the Busby family, but George preferred to be independent.

George Best was undoubtedly one of the most gifted players in the history of the game. He had an almost limitless talent. Even the best players, though, can develop some faults. Mine may have been that I was too fiery and responded too quickly to provocation. If George did have a fault, it was that he developed a tendency to hang on to the ball too long.

The most telling move in the game is the one-two, and the best exponent of it that I saw was Alfredo di Stefano. He almost never tried to beat an opponent by dribbling. A quick pass and dart through the defence for the return was his method, and it worked time and again. Done properly it is almost impossible to stop by fair means. In Argentina in 1978 we saw the Brazilians trying to stop Argentina from playing this way by ignoring the ball and attempting to block the man making the pass and run, but of course that is a foul.

George had the ability to play marvellous one-twos, or to beat a man and then lay the ball off. He was such a brilliant dribbler, though, that he loved taking people on. Often he would go past two or three men before cracking the ball into the net from some incredible angle. That was fine when it came off, and it came off remarkably often, but there were times when it might have been better for him to play to other members of the team rather than trying to do so much himself.

I played with Di Stefano, Puskas and Eusebio; like Cruyff and Pele these were players who would always lay the ball off to a man in a better position. Instead of scoring one goal, Pele could have had a hat-trick in the World Cup Final against Italy in Mexico in 1970, but twice he laid the ball off to men in better positions, once for Carlos Alberto to score and once for Jairzinho. Cruyff would only beat a man if he had to, and of course Puskas gave me the ball to score for the Rest of the World at Wembley when he could have scored himself. George was certainly in the same class as these players, apart from that tendency to hang on to the ball, and because of it I believe he never became the greatest player in the world, which he could have been.

I remember getting greedy at school, and also when I first came into the professional game. Then I realised that the ball beats the man far quicker than the player beats his man. A friend once said to me, 'Think of the other fellow as yourself when you pass to him, because you are really passing to him for yourself to score'. That was terrific advice because everyone is part of the team, and it doesn't really matter who scores the goals as long as someone does.

The arrival of George Best in the team brought us a giant step nearer to completion of the rebuilding which Matt Busby was undertaking. Now, we began to get Nobby Stiles involved in stopping the opposition. I don't advocate copying the ultra-defensive tactics of the Italians, but it is obviously important to stop the opposition from scoring. It is essential to have a sound defence: then you have something to build on. Pat Crerand and Nobby Stiles gave us a good blend in that way, one stopping, the other creating. With Nobby to cover for him, Pat's creative ability was released to produce more ammunition for the men up front, where, in addition to David Herd and myself, we now had George Best.

Then, of course, there was Bobby Charlton coming through with ferocious shots from midfield. He and David Herd were two tremendous strikers of the ball and whenever I saw either of them shaping up to shoot I would try to get in close to the goalkeeper – because I reckoned that even if he got a hand to the ball, he probably wouldn't be able to hold on to it. I scored a good many goals for United in that way, picking up the rebounds.

Two lads who looked like figuring in our long-term plans were Phil Chisnall and Ian Moir, both regular members of the side during that 1963–64 season. Both showed tremendous promise, but unfortunately neither fulfilled it. Chisnall eventually went to Liverpool, to play for Bill Shankly, but even there he failed to live up to expectations.

Early in 1964 I was appointed team captain when Noel Cantwell lost his place in the side to his Eire international colleague, Tony Dunne. Up to then, Noel had been captain, but he could hardly continue in the job when he was out of the team. He was such a fine natural leader though, and commanded so much respect among the players, that Matt Busby thought up the novel idea of making Noel club captain, while I captained the team on the field.

As the season wore on we found ourselves in the position of chasing three trophies, something which was to become a familiar pattern for English clubs in the coming years. We were well placed in the league, were in the quarter-finals of the European Cup-Winners' Cup, and had reached the semi-final of the FA Cup. As the fixtures piled up, the task became almost impossible and in the end we won none of the three.

Our FA Cup run began while I was under suspension. In the third round, we met our previous season's semi-final opponents, Southampton, and eventually won 3–2 after Saints had taken an early

2–0 lead. *My* first involvement in the Cup came in the fourth round, when we beat Bristol Rovers 4–1 and I scored three of the goals. Next we beat Barnsley 4–0, then came a marathon sixth round tie against Sunderland, which was to cost us dearly. The first match was at Old Trafford where we were 3–1 down, and within six minutes of defeat, before goals by Charlton and Best earned us a replay at Roker Park. Twice in that match we were behind, but we eventually drew 2–2 after extra time to earn a second replay at Leeds Road; the home of my first club, Huddersfield Town. Once again Sunderland scored first, but this time we blasted back to some purpose and won the match 5–1, including another hat-trick for yours truly. United were in an FA Cup semi-final for the third year in succession, but the effect of that drawn-out tie was to ruin our chances in both Cup competitions.

The FA Cup semi-final, against West Ham United, came only five days after our second replay against Sunderland. On league form we should have paralysed them, but after the marathon against Sunderland we were jaded. On a heavy, rain-soaked Hillsborough pitch we went down 3–1. Five days later we met Sporting Club of Lisbon in the second leg of the Cup-Winners' Cup quarter-final, in Lisbon. The first leg, at Old Trafford, had been one of our easiest European victories. We had beaten them 4–1, but it might have been ten. They had tried to restrict us by playing an offside game which proved to be fatal. Time and again we broke their offside trap and only a succession of bad misses and shots against the woodwork kept the score down to four. We had won the match so easily that the return leg seemed a formality. Lisbon were one of the poorest European teams I had seen, or so I thought. After I had hit a post early in the return game, we suddenly found that they were quite a decent side going forward. At old Trafford they had been content to defend and nothing had been seen of their forwards. Playing at home their tactics were different, and their front men turned out to be very lively indeed. Soon it was raining goals and in the end we were lucky to get away with a 5–0 thrashing.

Without taking anything away from Sporting Lisbon, there is no doubt that their victory over us owed as much to our ridiculous fixture pile-up as it did to their ability. In three weeks we had played two legs of the quarter-final tie against them, three sixth round FA Cup ties against Sunderland, and one FA Cup semi-final and an important league match, both against West Ham. *Seven* major matches in the space of just twenty-one days. That is the price which successful English clubs have always had to pay for their success, and still do.

The rest of Europe think we are mad. No other European country has a programme which puts its successful teams under such unreasonable pressure. The Italians wouldn't dream of asking teams to play the number of matches we do. They treat their players like racehorses. It was the effect of such massive fixture congestion which brought the squad system to England. Leeds United were the first club to realise fully that to compete in Europe, at the same time as competing on the domestic front, required not twelve or thirteen players, but a squad of sixteen or eighteen. Manchester United, Leeds, Liverpool, West Ham, Chelsea, Manchester City, Newcastle, Spurs and Nottingham Forest have all won European trophies, but I believe that our success should have been far greater and come sooner than it did. I believe that an English club should have won the European Cup earlier than 1968. United themselves should have won it in 1966.

English clubs will continue to find it difficult to be successful on both the domestic and European fronts simultaneously until the League is reduced in number and teams are asked to play far fewer matches. As things stand at present, provided he keeps clear of injury, a top international player with a successful English club can be asked to play in as many as sixty-odd matches in a season and that is far too many. No one can be expected to maintain a consistently high standard under those conditions.

I refer to English clubs, because of course the situation is different in Scotland, as it is elsewhere in Europe. There, not only do smaller leagues mean that teams play fewer matches, but also, because there are fewer good teams, even the matches they play are generally not as demanding. English clubs have a far tougher programme than any other country in Europe.

Having lost out in the two Cup competitions, we were left with just the league championship to play for. Our main rivals were the very good Liverpool side of St John, Hunt, Yeats, and company, which Bill Shankly had brought out of the second division only two seasons previously. The crunch came when we met them at Anfield in April, when we really needed to win to stay in the race. They beat us 3–0 and went on to take the title by four points. United were runners-up. The following year we had revenge when, again in April, we beat them 3–0 at Old Trafford on the way to winning the championship ourselves. In the middle sixties Liverpool and Manchester United came to monopolise the league championship, and it always seemed to work out that whoever came out best in our league meetings went on to win the title. Liverpool won it in 1964 and 1966, and we won it in 1965 and 1967.

Failing to win any of the three competitions was a great disappointment, but considering that the previous year we had very nearly been relegated, 1963–64 had to be judged a successful season. Runners-up in the league, FA Cup semi-finalists and European Cup

Winners' Cup quarter-finalists seemed a fair achievement. Although we hadn't quite made it this time, we had started to play really well, and were now clearly on the verge of winning a major trophy. We had sampled European football; it was good – the jam on the bread.

After Lisbon we were keen to get back into Europe, and by finishing runners-up in the league we had qualified for the following season's Inter-Cities Fairs Cup. We could approach the start of the 1964–65 season with a high degree of optimism.

CHAPTER 7

League Champions!

I reached an important milestone in my life when my first child, Gary, was born on 21 June 1964. When the new season began on 22 August there was also another new face in the United line-up. Few teams ever came to Old Trafford and won, but eighteen months previously we had been thrashed at home, 5–2, by Burnley. The star of that performance was their right-winger, John Connelly. He was our missing link. Right-wing was a position in which United still had a problem and Matt Busby solved it by paying out £56,000 for Connelly at the end of the 1963–64 season.

By an odd coincidence John made his league debut for United against West Bromwich Albion, the same team against which both George Best and I had first worn the red shirt. John had already made a good impression scoring two goals against Hamburg in a pre-season friendly in Germany. His arrival gave the team balance. With Connelly and Best, we now had two top quality wingers, giving us width. We had David Herd and myself in the middle, with Bobby Charlton making surging runs from midfield. Nobby Stiles and Pat Crerand provided a pivot between defence and attack, and behind them was a reliable rearguard of Shay Brennan and Tony Dunne, with Bill Foulkes at centre-half. David Gaskell was in goal at the start of the season, but he was later replaced by Pat Dunne who joined us from Shamrock Rovers.

For the first time since I had arrived at Old Trafford we now had what could be called a settled team. It took the new formation a couple of weeks to knit together, but after taking only five points from our first six matches of the season, we then had a run of fourteen league matches in which we dropped only one point. Our best result in this period was a 7–0 victory over Aston Villa, at Old Trafford, and in addition to our league performances we also disposed of Djurgaarden and Dortmund from the Fairs Cup with aggregate scores of 7–2 and 10–1 respectively. By the end of November, with twenty league matches played, we had taken thirty-two points from a possible forty. We led the first division by three points, with Tommy Docherty's

Chelsea in second place.

Playing for a winning side was a marvellous new experience. It was something I was going to get used to over the next few seasons, as United reached the peak of their powers. People used to ask, 'How can this United keep going? They've no tactics. Everything is played off the cuff'. That became our reputation but it wasn't strictly true. We did have tactics up to a point. We had people who marked at corner-kicks and throw-ins. We also had set free-kicks and corner-kicks. Apart from that though, Matt Busby's attitude was 'go out and play the football you know you can play. If you come off the field on your knees having been beaten, that's unlucky, but more often than not you'll come off winning if you adopt that attitude'. It looked as if we played it off the cuff because our tactics were flexible.

If our front men were being marked we would switch positions, which confused our opponents. The opposing right full-back might have been told to mark George Best but when George popped up on the right-wing, the full-back wouldn't know what to do. Similarly, if I was having a hard time against the centre-half, I would move out to the wing and George would come inside. We did this for a couple of years before managers started to tell defenders to simply pick up the nearest man, whoever it happened to be. One team which really did employ man-marking was Arsenal. Against them your marker would follow you all over the field. We managed to combat that by retreating towards our own half. Once defenders got too near to the halfway line they weren't sure what to do. Then we'd have Bobby breaking quickly from deep positions. The whole beauty of our game was its simplicity: skilful players using their heads and playing within the framework of a broad tactical plan. Regimentation is by definition predictable, and in the end the truly skilful players will always find a way to beat it.

In the early part of that 1964–65 season, violence off the field and discipline on it were subjects very much on the minds of the game's administrators. The FA had announced that they would be taking a tough new line against offenders, and the FA Secretary, Denis Follows, even spoke on one occasion about bringing in half-season bans. Trust me, then, to find myself once again on the wrong side of authority at such an inadvisable moment.

The trouble occurred when we met Blackpool in a league match at Bloomfield Road. They had a young-up-and-coming player in their side named Alan Ball. He seemed to have been given the job of marking me and followed me all over the field. We clashed once or twice and eventually I was booked for a foul on him. The referee was a Mr Peter Rhodes from York; a man I had never met. That was hardly surprising, since I wasn't particularly friendly with referees. To me they were just a part of the game. They had their job to do and I had mine. There was no reason for me to have anything to do with them socially and I didn't. My subsequent experiences with Mr Rhodes did nothing to make me feel that I should. As the referee was writing my name in his book, Pat Crerand came across to tell me to calm down. I wasn't feeling too pleased at that moment so I gave him a mouthful and the next thing I knew Mr Rhodes had ordered me off the field. Apparently, he thought that my remarks to Pat had been addressed to him.

It was an absolutely stupid way to get sent off but there was nothing I could do about it so I had to walk. The big question now concerned the punishment I was likely to be given. In the current atmosphere anything was possible. There was great speculation at the time that the FA was going to 'make an example of Law'. Because of the atmosphere and the way in which my sending off had occurred, I asked for a personal hearing, at which Pat Crerand gave evidence on my behalf. The disciplinary committee were not too impressed with my story, and I was given another twenty-eight day suspension plus a £50 fine. Thinking about it now, I suppose I was lucky that it wasn't more, but equally, in all fairness, I was being severely punished for having been the victim of circumstances as much as anything. For the second year in succession I was destined to spend Christmas at home in Aberdeen, but I hadn't planned it that way as some people seemed to think.

Having been suspended, this time I was allowed to go to the ground after Christmas to resume training in readiness for my return. I was still not getting paid though, and a group of the players got together to organise a whip round on my behalf. News of this got into the newspapers and the next thing we knew the FA were trying to stop it. Such a collection, they said, would be 'morally indefensible'. It was typical of them to stick their noses into things which didn't really concern them. If the lads had wanted to have a collection for me there was no way that the FA could have stopped it. As it was, everyone thought better of the idea and no money ever changed hands.

Shortly after my hearing, Rhodes was in trouble with the FA himself. Apparently he had leaked confidential information from the hearing to a Sunday newspaper. He was ordered to give an undertaking 'not to repeat conduct likely to bring the game into disrepute'. Some years later I bumped into him at Barcelona airport when my wife and I were on holiday in Spain. I went into the men's cloakroom and there was this familiar-looking chap standing next to me. He recognised me immediately and, to my amazement, boasted to me that he had made £7,000 out of stories he had given to the newspapers concerning trouble he had had with me and Malcolm Allison. 'I made a lot of money out of you', he said. I could hardly believe his cheek. That chance encounter put a damper on my holiday. I couldn't get his words out of my mind. I had lost nearly £1,000 in wages and bonuses, and he was boasting about having made £7,000 out of it.

Ironically, seven days after the start of my suspension it was anounced that I had been voted European Footballer of the Year. The award wasn't as well publicised in those days as it is today, but it was nevertheless a very great honour, and one of which I am proud. The only other British player to have received it at that time was Sir Stanley Matthews. Later on, of course, both George Best and Bobby Charlton won the same award, and in 1978 Kevin Keegan became the fifth British player to do so.

By the time I returned after suspension, we had moved into the new year and United were again chasing three trophies. We had been overtaken in the league by a Leeds United side which Don Revie had brought out of the second division only the previous season. No one realised it when the season began, but Leeds were at the start of a run which was to see them among the country's leading teams for the next decade. One of my last matches before suspension was their visit to Old Trafford for a league match in December. They caused the shock of the day by winning one-nil on a foggy afternoon when United did virtually all the attacking but couldn't get the ball into the net. Ten minutes from the end of the match the fog became so bad that the referee took the teams off the field, but to the dismay of our supporters he brought them back on again a few minutes later, for Leeds to complete their momentous victory. Leeds were taken much more seriously by everybody from that moment onwards, and meetings between us and them were to have great significance throughout the rest of that season, and for many seasons to come.

Because I had been able to train during my suspension, I was fully fit and raring to go when I made my reappearance in a league match against Nottingham Forest, at the City Ground on 16 January. Forest were one of the teams in the title race and I was delighted to score both of our goals in a 2–2 draw which gave us a valuable away point. The first goal came after only three minutes, and demonstrated my point that we did have a degree of planning and prepared moves in our play. We were awarded a free kick outside the penalty area which I shaped to take, but then ran over the ball leaving it for Bobby to knock to David Herd. I ran through the defence to receive David's accurate flick and a move which had worked like a perfect one-two ended with the ball in the back of Peter Grummit's net. We had scored an almost identical goal in the first round of the Fairs Cup against the Swedish side, Djurgaarden.

Just like the UEFA Cup, which succeeded it, the Inter-Cities Fairs

Cup was a very tough competition; perhaps the hardest of the three major European trophies to win. Instead of having just one top team from each country, there were normally two or three. Often a team who finished second or third in their domestic competition one season would go on to win it the following year, exactly as we were going to do. This meant that there might easily be two or three champions-elect among the entry for the Fairs Cups. Also because there were so many teams in it, the competition went on until well into the summer.

In 1965 we were still playing the semi-final in the middle of June. Having beaten Djurgaarden and Dortmund in the first two rounds, we met Everton in the third. They were quite a powerful side at that time. They had won the league championship in 1963 and finished third in 1964, just one point below United. In 1966 they went on to win the FA Cup.

We had two tremendous Fairs Cup matches against them. The first at Old Trafford ended 2–2, which seemed to give them the edge, but three weeks later at Goodison Park we beat them 2–1 to go through to meet Strasbourg in the quarter-final. We sewed that up by winning 5–0 in France, but the return leg was a rather disappointing goalless draw. Before the match at Old Trafford the French magazine, *France Football*, presented me with the six-inch diameter golden football which marks the award of European Footballer of the Year. It was a proud moment and I was only sorry that we couldn't manage a couple of goals in front of our own fans to celebrate the occasion in style. Still, we were through to the semi-final of a European competition, where we were to meet Ferencvaros of Hungary, one of the strongest teams in Europe.

Ferencvaros were not only the strongest physical side we had met, they were also a very good footballing side, whose star player was the Hungarian international centre-forward, Florian Albert. Also in their line-up, at inside-forward, was Zoltan Varga, who years later wound up playing for Aberdeen after having broken away from the Hungarian party during a tour of America, where he was given political asylum.

Our first meeting with Ferencvaros was at Old Trafford on the last day in May. David Herd scored two goals and I scored a third in United's 3–2 victory. The following week we went to Budapest for the return leg and a journey that I will remember for the rest of my life. Because of the peculiarities of Hungarian security, our flight from Manchester was not allowed to land in Budapest. Instead we had to land in Vienna, in Austria, and complete the remainder of the journey by coach. The distance between the two cities was only about a hundred miles, but of course we had to cross the border between the two countries. We were held up at the check point for more than two hours while Hungarian security people satisfied themselves that it was safe to let us enter. I think they were reasonably happy about the players and the club officials, but they were not so happy about some of the journalists who were travelling with us.

We had already driven some distance along the border fence, and sitting there waiting to cross gave us an opportunity to have a good look at it. It stretched for miles and miles. A double barrier of barbed-wire fencing with a few feet of no-man's-land between the two sections. Every two hundred yards or so there was a gun-turret manned by soldiers armed with machine-guns. It was just like a scene from a war-film, the only difference being that this was for real; *and* in peacetime. I'd seen a similar set-up in Poland. What sort of system of government, I wondered, was so marvellous that it was necessary to go to such lengths to keep people in?

Eventually we did reach Budapest, where we lost the semi-final second leg 1–0. That meant that the result of the tie was a 3–3 aggregate draw. There was no 'away goals' rule in those days, so Matt Busby agreed to toss a coin for home advantage in the replay. The two matches between us had been so tight that home advantage was likely to be crucial, and so it proved. Matt lost the toss, and we lost the replay 2–1. John Connelly scored our only goal in the match which was played on 15 June 1965. Ferencvaros went on to win the Fairs Cup by beating Juventus 1–0 in the final.

Losing to Ferencvaros brought our second semi-final defeat of the 1964–65 season. We had previously lost the FA Cup semi-final to Leeds United. That match too had gone to a replay. In the earlier rounds we disposed of Chester, Stoke, Burnley and Wolves; then came the semi-final at Hillsborough on 27 March – United's fourth FA Cup semi-final in successive seasons. It was a dreadful match. Semi-finals are always tense affairs because of what is at stake. In this one the tension boiled over in the first few minutes when there was a tremendous flare-up involving Jackie Charlton and myself, and several players from both sides. I don't really remember what started it, but it set the tone for a dour match which ended in a goalless draw.

I think that the blame for that brawl at Hillsborough probably belonged as much with one side as it did with the other. Both were capable of being a little aggressive and it would be unfair to try to suggest that the fault was all on their side. What is certain though is that Leeds were on their way to gaining a reputation for violence and cynicism which was to make them very unpopular throughout the game for the next decade. They had done remarkably well in their first season back in the first division, but unfortunately they were building their success on a pretty ruthless policy. They brought a new 'professional' attitude to the game, which seemed to be based on a philosophy of 'win at all costs'. Their tactics began to resemble a commando raid: knock out the main installations – which meant the key players – then get on with the job. They seemed to know which players were easily intimidated and which had fiery tempers and could be provoked.

There were always half a dozen men in the Leeds side ready and willing to do a demolition job where one was needed. Gamesmanship and the professional foul became their hallmark. I was rather surprised when Norman Hunter was selected by Alf Ramsey for England, because it seemed to give acknowledgement to those tactics. I had several clashes with Hunter, but I always felt that he was the sort of player who if you gave him a crack would go and look for somebody else to have a go at. If ever he did get into trouble with the referee, he would stand there with his hands behind his back like a schoolboy looking as if butter wouldn't melt in his mouth. Whenever any Leeds player had committed a bad foul, he would run forty or fifty yards away from the incident while other players crowded around the injured player and often, by the time he had sorted things out, the referee wouldn't know who the offender was.

One man in the Leeds side who earned a bit of an unfair reputation was Jack Charlton. He was a hard man but always fair. I think that his rather awkward appearance often made him look as though he was committing a foul when he really wasn't; as it did in the last minute of the World Cup Final against West Germany. Eddie Gray, Jimmy Greenhoff, Peter Lorimer and Mick Jones were also fair players, but these were exceptions to the general rule. Ironically, after doing all the damage that they did, Leeds eventually started to play some magnificent football in later years, but people in the game never forgave them for their earlier tactics.

Our semi-final replay against them was at Nottingham Forest's City Ground, four days after the battle of Hillsborough. I thought that we had had more than enough chances to win the first game, but the replay was even more frustrating. We paralysed them and had a bagful of chances but, although we hit the woodwork and just about every part of Gary Sprake's body, we couldn't get the ball into the net. We were just three minutes away from extra time when Giles sent a free-kick deep into our penalty area and Billy Bremner glanced the ball into our net off the back of his head. It was a goal which seemed to underline the fact that we were not destined to go to Wembley. Once again, Leeds had turned us over. They had already beaten us in the League, at Old Trafford, and were starting to become our bogey team.

Our chance for revenge came when we met them in the return league match, at Elland Road, in the middle of April. With just a handful of matches to play, they were three points ahead of us at the top of the league. We simply had to beat them if we were to stay in the title race with a real chance. By then we were beginning to think that we never would beat them, but, in a desperately hard-fought match, John Connelly scored the only goal to give us the two points we so badly needed. Two days later, on the following Monday, we went to St Andrews and beat Birmingham City 4–2, to go back to the top of the league table. We were now within sight of the championship.

Monday, 26 April 1965, was to be a memorable night. We were meeting Arsenal at home in our second-to-last match of the season. On the same evening Leeds were playing their last league match of the season, away to Birmingham City. Five days later they were due to meet Liverpool in the FA Cup Final at Wembley. Our superior goal average meant that three points from our last two matches would give us the title. If Leeds dropped a point at Birmingham, then a win over Arsenal would do it. It's a day I remember well because I hadn't expected to be playing. I had gashed my knee against Liverpool on the previous Saturday and had half a dozen stitches in the wound. That Monday lunchtime I was just about to hobble out of the ground when Matt Busby called me to say that it was time for the team talk. I said in amazement, 'What are you talking about? I've got half-a-dozen stitches in my knee, I can't play'. He said, 'Oh, you'll be all right, we'll get it strapped up. You're playing'. So I had to play. As it turned out, it was all right, my knee *was* well strapped up and the stitches remained intact. In the end I was glad that I did play because I scored a couple of goals in our 3–1 win, which turned out to be the clincher.

A tremendous roar went up when the news came through from St Andrews that Leeds were losing 3–0. All through the evening we kept hearing news of the progress of that match as the score changed: 1–3, 2–3, and finally 3–3. That was it. With just one match to play we were level with Leeds on points and they had completed their programme. Aston Villa would have to beat us by double figures in our one remaining match if Leeds were to finish with a better goal average than ours. As it happened, we did lose to Villa, two nights later, but only by two goals to one. Leeds' disappointment was completed on the Saturday when, after extra time, they lost the FA Cup Final to Liverpool. For them a season which had promised so much had ended leaving them empty-handed. The previous season we had had that experience, but now it was champagne time at Old Trafford. Matt Busby's rebuilding had reached a point of fulfilment. United were once again League Champions. Even more significantly for Matt, I'm sure, just over

even years after Munich we had again qualified for the European
Cup.

I wonder what memories were conjured up for him on that night?
After the trauma of all that had happened, our achievement must have
given him immense satisfaction.

CHAPTER 8

Transfer Listed

Goalscoring forwards are the players most prone to injury. The striker is continually up at the sharp end and must be prepared to go in where it hurts. No striker doing his job properly is likely to complete a full season of forty-two league matches; he is bound to spend a fair proportion of his time on the treatment table. There is no telling at the time whether the knocks he takes will simply be temporarily painful, or whether they might have a more permanent consequence. In the heat of battle, knocks are given and taken and only afterwards is the cost counted. I had my fair share of knocks over the years, and the worst occurred when I was playing for Scotland against Poland, in a World Cup qualifying match at Hampden Park. A kick on the kneecap which I received in that match began an injury saga which was to last for the remainder of my playing days.

In the qualifying stage for the 1966 World Cup Finals, Scotland were drawn in a group with Finland, Poland and Italy. As the host nation, England did not have to qualify. Scotland's first qualifying match was against Finland, at Hampden Park, in October 1964. We got off to a good start with a 3–1 victory, with goals from Chalmers, Gibson and myself. Seven months later we achieved a particularly good result when we held Poland to a 1–1 draw in Chorzow, where I scored our only goal; then we had a second win over Finland, this time by 2–1 in Helsinki. We had taken five points from a possible six, so when we met Poland for a second time at Hampden Park on 21 October 1965 Scottish optimism was running high.

No one can legislate for luck, and it turned out to be one of those infuriating matches where we had almost total domination but couldn't score the goals which our superiority warranted. After spending eighty-five minutes virtually camped in the Polish half of the field, all we had to show for our efforts was a single goal scored by Billy McNeill. Then, in the last five minutes of the match, Poland scored twice from breakaways. One moment we had been coasting to victory, the next we had lost. It was a result with a remarkable parallel in the one where England met Poland at Wembley in 1973. Just as England's failure then to win a match they had totally dominated prevented them from qualifying for the 1974 World Cup Finals, so our defeat a Hampden Park went a long way towards keeping us out of the Finals of 1966.

Only after the match did I become fully conscious of the pain in my knee. Of course, it had hurt like hell when it had happened, but at the time it was no different from a thousand and one other knocks which are all part and parcel of the game. After the match it was still very sore. It was a rule at Old Trafford that players who received injuries in international matches *must* report to the ground for treatment on the day immediately following the match. My knee was still painful the following morning, but because I had missed the early flight from Glasgow to Manchester I disobeyed the club rules. By the time I did arrive at Old Trafford, on Friday morning, the team were reporting for travel to London where we were playing Spurs on the following day. In the circumstances I didn't think it wise to make too much fuss about my injury, so I kept quiet. The match at White Hart Lane was a night mare. Jimmy Greaves scored a memorable goal and we were annihil ated 5–1. By half-time the pain in my knee was so bad that I didn't turn out for the second half. That was the start of an injury which was finally going to result in an operation two and a half years later in 1968. From then on I would never be completely free from pain in my right knee.

In the mid-sixties the Scottish press were violently anti-Anglo. Any non-resident Scot had to be twice as good as a player playing in Scot land to win their approval. Things have improved quite a lot in recent years, but after our defeat by Poland in 1965 my name was mud in the Scottish newspapers. The knives were out in a big way. Even so, I was surprised and very disappointed to be dropped from the squad for our next qualifying match, against Italy, the following month. Scotland still had a slender chance of qualifying if we could beat Italy twice. Although I wasn't playing I was delighted when we did beat them 1–0 at Hampden Park. This meant that our final match, in Naples on December, would be crucial. The odds against any team winning in Italy are never more than slender at the best of times but, to my great delight, I was back in the squad and all set to make a comeback when got a kick on the shin in United's league match against West Ham on the Saturday before the international.

Jock Stein had come down from Scotland to watch the match and to check on my form and fitness, but it was obvious after I had received the injury that I would not be fit to play for Scotland. I had what the medical profession calls a haematoma. We actually let the press lads see the large swelling on my leg so that there would be no suggestion in

On international duty with my new friend, Tommy Docherty.

Left: Stripped for action in my childhood.

Below: An Aberdeen Schoolboys XI —Alex Dawson holding the cup, yours truly kneeling on the right at the end of the front row. (*R. Broome*)

A training session with Bill Shankly in the early days at Huddersfield.
(*Manchester Daily Mail*)

Being pursued by the great Sivori in the match between Juventus and
Torino which Torino won 1–0, with a goal by Joe Baker.

Joe Baker and I enjoying one of the lighter moments of our Italian adventure.

The wreck of the car in which Joe and I almost lost our lives.

My Italian ordeal is over: signing for Manchester United flanked by Gigi Peronace, Jimmy Murphy and Matt Busby.

Gordon Banks takes the ball away from my feet during the 1963 FA Cup Final between Manchester United and Leicester City. (*Syndication International*)

A few words of friendly advice from referee Jack Taylor. (*Syndication International*)

Playing for Scotland against Zaire in the 1974 World Cup Finals. (*Syndication International*)

One goal I almost wished I hadn't scored—I (number 10) back-heel the ball past Alex Stepney and into United's net during the last match of my league career. (*County Press Photos*)

My own team of Scottish superstars. (*R. Broome*)

anyone's mind that I was ducking the match in Italy. I don't suppose for one moment that my presence would have made any difference, but it's a matter of record now that Scotland were beaten 3–0. Italy were through to the World Cup Finals; Scotland were out. That was the first blow in a season which was going to get worse before it was over.

Being the English league champions means that every match you play resembles a cup-tie. Everyone wants to beat you, and very few teams have managed to retain the title for a second successive year. Since the advent of European football, the task has become even harder. Playing in the European Cup and trying at the same time to re-tain the English title is an almost impossible task which only Liverpool have managed to achieve when they completed that momentous double in 1977. In the 1965–66 season our league form was not bad, but never good enough for us to retain the title. It was clear that if we were going to win anything it would be one of the cups. Not that we ever decided we weren't going to bother about the league – that doesn't happen in football – but it did seem to happen that our best results were in cup-ties. I think also that our league form suffered as a result of the number of important matches we had to play. Some of our worst league results came after we had returned from mid-week fixtures in Europe. Our away matches against Helsinki, Benfica and Partizan, for instance, were all followed by league defeats on the Saturday; at Arsenal, Chelsea and Sheffield United respectively.

I suppose that the competition we most wanted to win was the European Cup – and we should have won it. In the early rounds we disposed of Helsinki and the East German side, ASK Vorwaerts, then found our-selves paired with the favourites, Benfica, in the quarter-final. Benfica were among the cream of Europe at the time: European Cup finalists four times in the previous five seasons, and winners of the trophy twice in that period. No one wanted to meet Benfica in the quarter-final. If we could beat them, then we should be able to beat anyone else in the tournament.

The first leg was at Old Trafford, where after half an hour Augusto gave Benfica the lead. Goals by David Herd, myself and Bill Foulkes then swept *us* into a 3–1 lead, until late in the game Torres pulled the score back to 3–2. That seemed to leave us with too much to do in Lisbon, where a single goal lead was likely to be swallowed up very quickly. Benfica were unbeaten in seven years of European football in their own 'Stadium of Light', and our last visit to Lisbon had ended in a five-nil thrashing at the hands of their neighbours, Sporting Club. The Portuguese supporters were determined that we shouldn't forget that disastrous night two seasons earlier, and as our coach edged its way through the throng towards the stadium they crowded round in their thousands to hold up five fingers at the windows.

What an irony, then, that this time it was our turn to score five in a 5–1 victory, which will always rank as one of the outstanding performances by a British club in Europe. Before the match everything seemed to be conspiring against us. Eusebio had been voted European Footballer of the Year in 1965 and we were kept waiting while he was presented with the trophy. When Mr Lobello did finally get the match under way twenty minutes late, rockets roared into the night sky and there weren't too many among the eighty thousand crowd who were cheering for United.

Nevertheless, we had the match won in fifteen minutes with two goals from Georgie Best and one from John Connelly. Bobby Charlton and Pat Crerand added two more in the second half. That was the night when we put it all together. It was a brilliant team performance, but the man who had really caught the imagination of the football world was George Best. His early two-goal blast had shattered Benfica almost single-handed. The following day the Portuguese press christened him *El Beatle* and from that moment on his life was never the same. The result was acclaimed across Europe, and amid all the euphoric press reports one quote in the Portuguese newspaper *Seculo* expressed things particularly succinctly. It said, simply, 'A notable exhibition by Manchester. But after all, wasn't it the British who invented football?'.

After beating Benfica, United were favourites to become the first British club to win the European Cup, but incredibly we lost the semi-final to an unknown team named Partizan of Belgrade.

The seeds of that defeat may well have been sewn before ever we met our Jugoslav opponents. Our FA Cup campaign that season began at the Baseball Ground, where we thrashed Derby County 5–2. In the fourth round we needed two attempts to dispose of second division Rotherham United. After a goalless draw at Old Trafford, an extra-time goal by John Connelly settled the replay at Millmoor. We beat Wolves 4–2 in the fifth round tie at Molyneux, after conceding two penalties in the first nine minutes and being two goals down. Then, in the sixth round, we drew 1–1 with Preston North End, at Deepdale, and won the replay 3–1 at Old Trafford. United had created a record by reaching the semi-final of the FA Cup for the fifth year in succession, but the cost was to prove high. In our first meeting with Preston, George Best had been brought down from behind and had aggravated a cartilage injury in his right knee, which had been troubling him for some time. It was ironic that he and I should be suffering the same injury, although at the time no one realised that my problem was a cartilage. Cartilages can sometimes be nursed for a little while, and in the hope that George might last out the season it was announced that he had strained a ligament. It was a pious hope which was doomed to failure.

April 1966 was a bad month. It began with Scotland losing 4–3 to England at Hampden Park. As Scotland were not qualified for the World Cup Finals and England were, we would dearly have loved to have beaten them, but it was not to be. To be fair we were slightly flattered by the closeness of the score. My only consolation was in scoring one of our goals. For United, April was the month when once again we were to find the pressure of too many important matches in too short a space of time an impossible burden.

In the space of ten days our hopes of the European and FA Cups lay in ruins. It all began when we met Partizan in Belgrade on the thirteenth of the month. Further knee trouble had kept me out of our league match against Leicester City on the previous Saturday, and with George Best playing with his right knee strapped up, neither of us was one hundred per cent fit in Belgrade. In fact George broke down and required treatment during the game, which was to be his last appearance of the season. Even so, we should still have beaten this very ordinary Partizan side. Early in the game George sent over a cross which needed only to be side-footed into the net. I was about two yards from the goal line, but I completely missed the ball which bounced off my thigh and on to the crossbar. Soon after that dreadful miss, Partizan scored. The effect of taking the lead was a real stimulant to them, and with their crowd getting behind them they eventually scored a second to win the match 2–0.

We hadn't played well. After conceding that early goal we had always been struggling. Two goals are a lot to pull back in any European competition, but we were still confident that we could win the tie at Old Trafford. When the teams met again, a week later, we were without George Best, the man who had tamed Benfica. It was a night of tremendous tension on and off the field. We were just one step away from the European Cup Final. Old Trafford was bursting at the seams and the crowd was urging us on. Somehow though we seemed to be trying almost too hard and, although we completely dominated the game, all we had to show for our domination at the end of ninety minutes was a late goal scored by Nobby Stiles. What really hurt was that, apart from the minnows you get in the early rounds, Partizan were unquestionably one of the poorest sides we had met in Europe and yet they had beaten us by an aggregate of 2–1. Our victory over Benfica seemed a thing of distant memory.

We hardly had time to recover from that disappointment before we were due to meet Everton in the FA Cup semi-final at Burnden Park three days later. Unlike us, they had not had to play two European semi-finals in the previous ten days. Even so, they had felt it wise to field practically a reserve side for the league match against Leeds United the previous Saturday, for which they were later fined £2000 by the Football League. I don't suppose they minded that too much though because by then they were in the FA Cup Final, which they won by beating Sheffield Wednesday 3–2. The match at Burnden Park was a very scrappy game in which neither side created many chances and Colin Harvey scored the goal which gave Everton their one-nil victory.

Once again we had fallen at the final hurdle. We had lost both of our semi-finals by a single goal. So near, and yet so far. Not for the first time, a season which had started so full of promise had yielded nothing at the end. We had no hope of retaining the title which was once again bound for Liverpool. Although we did finish our league programme with a bit of a flourish, we still only managed fourth place in the league table, which was not high enough to qualify us for a place in Europe the following season. We had won nothing and had nothing to look forward to, and what made it worse from a Scots point of view, England were about to play host to the World Cup. It promised to be a depressing summer.

A few days before the World Cup Finals were due to begin, Matt Busby rocked the football world by announcing that he had put me on the transfer list. He said that I had given the club a written ultimatum which they could not accept and so they were prepared to release me. At the time my contract was due for renewal and I *had* written to Matt asking for a signing-on fee and an increase in wages. I had also said that if I didn't get what I wanted I would ask for a move. I suppose it was a bit strong, but I didn't really want to leave and I'm sure that Matt knew that. What I did want of course was more money. I was a bit disappointed by the way Matt reacted. I was in Aberdeen at the time waiting with my wife for the birth of our second child. Matt received my letter on a Tuesday and replied to me the same day. In his reply he said that the club could not comply with my demands, and he invited me to get in touch with him to discuss it. The post up to Scotland is not quick and the following day, Wednesday, he released the story to the press before I had actually received his letter. I thought that he might have waited until I had had time to make contact with him; had he done so then nothing would have come out publicly because I was only trying him on.

I was having a quiet round of golf when the news broke. I'll never forget it. One moment the golf course was deserted, then all of a sudden the hordes came over the hill in the distance. It was like the charge of the light brigade. Before I knew where I was I was up to my neck in pressmen. The hit song of the day was the Beatles' number, *Yesterday* (all my troubles seemed so far away), and I remember thinking that they might have written it for me. I was forced to go into hiding for a couple of days, but when I eventually flew back to Manchester, to meet Matt, we soon had the problem sorted out and I signed a new contract on 30 June, exactly one week after being put on the transfer list. Three days later my wife gave birth to our second son, Andrew.

I think that the club had used me as an example. I don't believe that Matt ever wanted me to leave, but he had to show that the club is bigger than the individual. At the time there were one or two others who were dissatisfied with the wages structure. We knew that certain other clubs, such as Everton, Spurs and Leeds, were paying really good money and ours didn't seem good enough. Several other players were on the point of making a protest, but I was the first one to do so. By knocking me on the head, the club had effectively nipped the thing in the bud. To the world at large it appeared that the club had won. It really was bigger than the player. What had actually happened was that we had compromised. I didn't get the signing-on fee I had asked for, but I did get an increase in wages. I've always said, regarding contracts, that it is up to each individual to get the best deal he can. Once you've signed a contract, don't moan. I never knew what other people got and they never knew what I got. That didn't matter so long as I was happy with my contract. On this occasion I hadn't got everything I had asked for, I didn't expect to, but at least I had got more than had originally been offered. Publicly the club had come out on top. Privately I was quite content with the way things had worked out. The one thing I had never wanted was to leave United.

One good thing about the summer of 1966, from my point of view, was that for the first time in six years I was able to have a bit of a break. I had been on the go virtually non-stop since leaving Huddersfield. Of course, I would have loved to have been playing for Scotland in the World Cup Finals, but our failure to qualify did at least give me the opportunity to take a sorely needed rest. The cumulative effect of so much football had begun to show during the 1965–66 season, both in the fact that I scored only fifteen league goals in thirty-three matches, and in the number of times I was injured. I was tired and Mr Glass, the specialist who had been looking into the trouble in my right knee, advised me to spend the summer fishing and playing golf.

I was actually on the golf course at Chorlton-cum-Hardy when England beat West Germany in the World Cup Final. I had purposely chosen that day to settle an outstanding golfing challenge against my friend, John Hogan, who has an engineering business in Manchester. We had struck up a bet of twenty-five pounds on a round of golf 'anytime, anywhere'. I elected to play on 30 July 1966, so that I would not have to watch the World Cup Final. While the clubhouse was packed with members watching the match on television, there were just two of us on the course. Normally I would have expected to beat John, but that day I couldn't do a thing right and I lost the bet. As we came round the corner from the eighteenth green a crowd of the members were at the clubhouse window cheering and waiting to tell me that England had won the World Cup. It was the blackest day of my life.

Why is there this tremendous rivalry from Scotsmen towards England? People often ask that question and I don't really know the answer, but I suspect that it has something to do with the little country against the bigger country. I know that the same rivalry exists between Northern Ireland and England, and between Wales and England; it's not just the Scots. When Alf Ramsey became England team manager I believe that he brought a little of the same feeling to the English attitude. I had three of England's World Cup squad to live with at Old Trafford – Bobby Charlton, Nobby Stiles and John Connelly – and after they had won the World Cup I knew that I would be hearing about nothing else for the next four years. We were team mates for United, but bitter rivals when it came to internationals. When a team wins the FA Cup the magic lasts for twelve months, until someone else wins the trophy. The World Cup comes round only once every four years. I couldn't wait for 1970 so that someone else would win it and take the spotlight off England.

Leaving national loyalties on one side, although England's victory in the World Cup Final was obviously a great achievement which at the time gave the game a badly needed boost, I think that in the long run it was a bad thing for British football. It was the beginning of the end of football as we knew it. We had seen the beautiful flowing attacking football of Spurs; now we had 4–3–3, a system without wingers. That was the worst thing that ever happened to the game, because it killed the art of scoring goals. You can't blame Ramsey for the decline of British football as a spectacle, you must blame the people who followed his example. He set the pattern and he was successful with it because he had the players to make it work. If every team had three front men like Hurst, Hunt and Ball, then they might have been successful too; but no team had. These three were the type of players who were prepared to do a lot of running – taking people out of position by making dummy runs and creating gaps. In place of wingers we had overlapping full-backs. It worked for a time for England, but it was going to be disastrous for the bread and butter stuff.

One of the first teams to adopt the new negative style were West Ham United, but it failed to bring them success. They had won the FA Cup in 1964 and the European Cup-Winners' Cup the following season, but from 1966 onwards despite having England's Bobby Moore, Geoff Hurst and Martin Peters in their side, they became a team who were always fighting for survival rather than one trying to win something.

To think that Jimmy Greaves was not picked for the World Cup Final, and that there were good wingers like John Connelly, Peter Thompson and Peter Brabrook sitting on the bench (England even had perhaps the best winger in the world – Bobby Charlton – playing in midfield) was a sin – sacrilege. I've always said that England only won the World Cup because they had six matches at home. Getting to the Final was all about getting results; about not getting beaten in the early rounds. All right, the system worked in that limited context for England, in favourable circumstances, but to play football like that on a permanent basis would be fatal. British football had always been about thrills. With no wingers, attacks were coming just from midfield, negative to watch and negative to play. You didn't need to be a Jimmy Greaves to play football like that. After 4–3–3, the next logical step was 4–4–2, where we now had four men in midfield. Then of course the system went back to the schools and everybody wanted to be a midfield player. I hoped that when Brazil won the World Cup in 1970 things might change, but for the first time that I could remember that didn't happen: teams didn't start to adopt the style of the World Champions. The reason was that they couldn't, because they hadn't got the players to make the change.

The year 1966 saw the start of eight or ten years of bad football. It took a couple of seasons to work its way thoroughly into the league system, but within a few years British football had become, for the most part, boring and predictable. Skill was being stifled at birth and I don't think it is any coincidence that there are not the same number of outstanding players around now as there used to be. One glimmer of hope in the last couple of seasons has been the renewed interest in wingers. Manchester United and Manchester City were two of the clubs who pioneered the way and since Ron Greenwood brought them back into the England side, players like Peter Barnes and Steve Coppell have suddenly become fashionable. It may only be a coincidence, of course, but since they started to adopt a more adventurous attacking policy, England's fortunes have improved tremendously.

CHAPTER 9

League Champions Again

During the 1965–66 season I was troubled many times by the pain in my right knee. I made several visits to the specialist and underwent a varied programme of treatment consisting of heat massage, injections and a system of electric shocks applied to the quadraceps known as Faradism. To all those who think that too much is made of footballers' injuries, I would simply say 'try it'. You lie there with two metal plates attached to your thigh and wait for the shocks to arrive at about five-second intervals. Believe me, it is painful.

The injury got worse as the season wore on, but after my summer of rest I was comparatively free from pain when the 1966–67 season began. As we had not qualified for any of the European competitions and were destined to make an early exit from both the league and FA Cups, this was to be our easiest season. No doubt because of that I got through until early December before the knee again started to give me problems. I actually began the season with a flourish, scoring twelve goals in eleven league matches, including two in each of our opening fixtures, against West Brom and Everton. The second of my two against Everton was my hundredth league goal for United, scored in a hundred and thirty-nine league games in just over four seasons.

In the early weeks of that season there were a number of changes to the team. One surprise was the rather sudden selling of John Connelly to Blackburn Rovers. I felt that he was made something of a scapegoat for our failure in the previous season's two semi-finals. He certainly hadn't done much against Partizan, and in the FA Cup semi-final at Burnden Park Everton's full-back, Sandy Brown, had played him out of the game. It was strange though, the suddenness with which he went. After all he had been a member of England's World Cup squad during the summer. I was sorry to see him go because, although he may not have been the bravest of players, he had done a good job for United. He had given us width, and was great at coming inside and having a crack at goal with his left foot. That often created goals from rebounds when he failed to score himself. The season before he was sold, John was United's leading European goalscorer with six of our twenty-three in the European Cup.

His departure made way for John Aston, a left-sided player, who played on the left-wing. That allowed George Best to switch to his more natural side on the right. Wingers usually get plenty of time to rest in a match and Matt Busby liked them to use it to pick up the opposing full-backs to prevent the goalkeeper throwing the ball to them. Besty was marvellous at that, and John Connelly had been good at it too. Aston was a straightforward player who did a job and came back to help the defence. I wouldn't say he was the cleverest of players. He certainly hadn't a great football brain and he didn't see the openings as quickly as Besty or Connelly. His arrival really made little difference to the pattern of our play which was still basically something of a 4–2–4 formation.

One important change in the early weeks of the season was the signing of a new goalkeeper – Alex Stepney. Although we had four goalkeepers on the books at that time, it was still a problem position. Harry Gregg suffered a variety of injuries, the worst of which was a nagging shoulder complaint which gave him great pain and prevented him from stretching properly. On the pre-season tour of 1966–67 he had three disastrous matches in which we conceded thirteen goals. That cost Harry his place in the side for the start of the season.

Our first tour match was away to Celtic where I think that Scottish determination to beat an English side was heightened by England's recent victory in the World Cup. They hammered us 4–1. Next we went to West Germany to play Bayern Munich, where determination to beat an English club after West Germany's defeat in the World Cup Final was probably even greater than it had been in Scotland. Again we were trounced 4–1. In our final tour match, against FK Austria, we were beaten 5–2, and we started the new season with Matt Busby desperately trying to find a successful formula, with David Gaskell back in goal. In mid-September David became yet another injury victim – and it was then that Matt paid out £55,000 for Alex Stepney. It was a lot of money for a goalkeeper and Matt was taking a bit of a gamble. Although Alex was an Under 23 international, his experience had all been gained in the third division. Chelsea had only recently bought him from Millwall to understudy Peter Bonnetti, and he had played in only one first division match when Chelsea's manager, Tommy Docherty, agreed to release him to United. A couple of days after he had signed, Alex and I sat in the stand at Bloomfield Road to watch United play Blackpool in a league cup tie. Pat Dunne had taken over from the injured David Gaskell for his first match of the season. United lost 5–1 and the following Saturday Alex Stepney made his debut against Manchester City. We won that match 1–0 with a goal which I scored. Later in the season Harry Gregg was transferred to Stoke and Dunne went to Plymouth Argyle. Our other goalkeeper, Jimmy Rimmer, was keeping a regular place in the reserves.

Other young players who were coming into the picture around that time were David Sadler, Willie Anderson, Jimmy Ryan, Francis Burns, Brian Kidd and my long-haired Aberdonian mate, John Fitzpatrick. He was a fiery midfield player who played in our first three matches of the season, then had to go into hospital to have the inevitable cartilage removed. Our best youngster though was Bobby Noble, a left full-back who, in my opinion, was destined to go right to the top, until a car accident ended his career later that season. He came into the side in November, after we had been beaten 4–1 by Johnny Carey's title-chasing Nottingham Forest. That result dropped us to eighth place in the league – our lowest position of the season – and Noble came into the side in the reshuffle that followed. He was yet another product of United's youth policy; a terrific prospect.

I think that in time Bobby would have taken over from Ray Wilson and been England's left-back for many years. He had a little bit of a chip on his shoulder, and was inclined to be a bit naughty. He liked to let players know he was there, and had no respect for anyone's reputation. I had some great tussles with him in five-a-side matches. He had a good football brain and was a good user of the ball. He read the game well, and for a young lad coming into the side with a lot of established players, he slotted in remarkably smoothly, just as though he had been there for years.

That is the perfect formula – to bring young players into a successful side, as, for instance, Liverpool do. Too many clubs bring youngsters in when the side is struggling and it really is hard for them to do well. Bobby Noble came into our side and was immediately at home. For me, Ray Wilson was the best left-back I ever saw and yet this boy Noble might have been better. He had that little nasty streak which is essential in a defensive player, and he had great confidence. What a tragedy that his career was cut short.

Noble came off the same assembly line which had earlier produced Nobby Stiles, who also had a reputation for having a bit of 'bite'. Actually Nobby was not a dirty player at all as some people thought, certainly not cold and calculating. He was like a little Scottish terrier. He was often given the job of marking an opposing player and did it particularly well. Alf Ramsey used him that way in the World Cup, when he did a first class job on Eusebio. Nobby was a wholehearted tackler and not unnaturally he would occasionally have fouls awarded against him, but he was never vindictive or vicious. He got a bit of a reputation during the World Cup which probably wasn't helped by his appearance: he certainly was a gruesome sight with his front teeth out.

Following our defeat at Nottingham, we had a run of eight matches from which we took fifteen points before losing again 2–1 to Aston Villa, at Villa Park. After that match I felt severe pain in my knee for the first time that season, and I was unfit for the visit of Liverpool to Old Trafford the following week. George Best scored our two goals in a 2–2 draw, which was of great importance in the championship race. A fortnight later, on 16 December, we suffered our last league defeat of the season when we were beaten 2–1 by Sheffield United, at Bramall Lane.

We had been beaten six times, but always away from home. At Old Trafford our record remained intact and we would not be beaten again in twenty league matches, home or away, on our run-in to the title. If we were invincible at home in the League, the same was not true of the FA Cup; our defeat at Old Trafford by Norwich City, in the fourth round, ranked as one of the shocks of the season. United had never failed to reach the semi-final stage in the five previous seasons and we started the Cup campaign well enough with a two-nil victory over Stoke City at Old Trafford. The one goal which I scored in that match was my thirty-first in FA Cup football (excluding the six I had scored for Manchester City in the abandoned match against Luton Town), which made me the highest goalscorer in the history of the competition. The record had previously been held jointly by Stan Mortensen, Ronnie Allen and John Atyeo with thirty goals apiece.

I was still two goals short of Jack Rowley's club record of twenty-eight FA Cup goals for United, but the one I scored in the next round, against Norwich, put me just one short of that total. Norwich City were struggling in the lower half of the second division when they came to Old Trafford and none of the football pundits gave them a price. But the history of the FA Cup is littered with shock results – they are part of its great appeal – and Norwich City provided one of the biggest by doing what no first division side could do at Old Trafford: they beat us 2–1.

At the time it seemed like a disaster, and one which was hard to explain. Laurie Brown, who played for Norwich that day, lambasted all the United players in the press for 'not trying'. The criticism seemed fair for most of us; it *was* our worst performance of the season. The only really valid explanation, though, must be that we approached the match far too casually. Once you lose your edge in football, it's difficult to get it back, no matter whom you are playing. As it happened, losing that match turned out to be the best thing that could have happened to us. We were all so disgusted by our own performance that the only way we could salvage some pride was by saying 'right, now let's go out and win the league title'. That was all there was left for us to win. In the three previous seasons we had lost trophies through the fixture congestion caused by chasing too many honours. Now the boot was on the other foot. With three and a half months of the season left to play, all we had in front of us were league matches.

Our most serious rivals were Spurs, Liverpool and the Nottingham Forest side of Terry Hennessy, Henry Newton and company, which was enjoying what was then the club's best season in the first division. Their visit to Old Trafford in the middle of February was a crucial one and we managed to beat them 1–0, with a goal scored five minutes from time by yours truly. A month earlier we had beaten Spurs at home by the same score and a month after beating Forest, we went to the top of the table after a goalless draw at St James's Park against Newcastle United. That was in the middle of March, and from then on we were never headed.

Exactly one week after the Newcastle match we beat Leicester City 5–2 at Old Trafford, but it was a victory tinged with sadness because David Herd broke his leg in scoring one of our goals. David was chasing a through ball, and as Gordon Banks came out of his goal, somehow he managed to dive underneath David's foot which he had stuck out to toe-poke the ball. At the same moment Graham Cross came in to tackle and fell down right on top of David's leg. There was a sickening crack which echoed around the stadium. Everyone in the ground knew what had happened. It sounded just like a pistol shot. I haven't seen many breaks, but that was a terrible mess. The bone was actually sticking through the sock.

Ironically the ball had ended up in the back of the net for David's sixteenth league goal of the season. It was the one hundred and thirteenth league goal he had scored in six seasons with the club, which shows what a valuable asset he had been. He wasn't a particularly skilful player, and he occasionally came in for a bit of criticism, but he had a tremendously powerful shot and was consistently on the target. In six seasons he was twice leading goalscorer and four times second to me. Unfortunately, as so often happens, the broken leg virtually ended his career. He did make a brief comeback the following season, but soon moved to Stoke and never really did anything much in the game after that.

For United, the loss of a goalscorer was a pretty serious blow, even though we did have one or two players in the side who could pop them in. Fortunately we were getting towards the end of the season, so the loss was not quite as serious as it might have been. We did have another centre-forward, David Sadler, who was often used as a centre-half. David was a good steady player, but not outstanding in either position. He was a good elegant mover, rather like Paul Madeley of Leeds. He lacked a yard of pace up front, where it was now getting more difficult to play, and he lacked the bit of devilment which is an essential part of the striker's make-up. As a defensive player he was a bit in the mould of John Charles but without having quite the same skill. David was a good utility player who did a reasonable job for United over a number of seasons.

A week after David Herd's injury we went to Anfield, and took another great step towards the title by holding Liverpool to a goalless draw. We now had nine matches left to play, all of them against teams in the lower half of the league table, and it was just a matter of keeping our heads and staying ahead of the field. This we did and finally settled the championship with an emphatic 6–1 win over West Ham United, at Upton Park, in our second-to-last match of the season. It was our biggest win of the season, home or away, and a fitting way to win the championship. Of our twenty-one home matches, we had won seventeen and drawn four, and we had taken thirty points from a possible forty from our last twenty league matches. We ended the season with sixty points, four more than Nottingham Forest and Spurs, each of whom had fifty-six.

As great a thrill as it was to win our second league championship in three years, the highlight of that season came for me not when I was playing for United, but when I played for Scotland against England at Wembley on 15 April 1967. Less than nine months earlier, in that very stadium, England had won the World Cup, and they were unbeaten since winning it. Matches against England always have a special significance for the Scots, but this one had a far greater significance than ever. We always seemed to do better at Wembley than when we played them at home. Somehow at Hampden Park the crowd seemed to get through to us and we didn't play well. At Wembley conditions were ideal for playing good football. We went out determined to show them and, although we had something of a makeshift team, we beat England 3–2, to become the first country to beat the reigning World Champions. The first goal came when Wallace had a shot which Gordon Banks couldn't hold and I got the rebound to continue my habit of scoring against Banksy at Wembley. Bobby Lennox made it 2–0 before Jackie Charlton pulled one back for England, but when Jim McCalliog made it 3–1 the match was as good as over. We were well on top by then and should have taken the opportunity to rub it in. Scotland never seemed to beat England by a big score and this was our opportunity to take revenge for the 9–3 thrashing we had suffered a few years earlier. The score could easily have been 4 or 5–1, but we allowed ourselves to relax instead of trying to get those extra goals.

Jim Baxter was a magnificent player, who had a great record against England. He had scored both of Scotland's goals in the 2–1 win on a previous visit to Wembley in 1963. This time, though, he started knocking the ball about instead of hammering home our advantage and we almost allowed England to wriggle off the hook; a goal by Geoff Hurst late in the game gave the final score a look of respectability which they hardly deserved. Still, we had beaten the World Champions, and the result would give me some respite. I could go back to Old Trafford confident in the knowledge that there would be no more mickey-taking by my English club-mates.

CHAPTER 10

Champions of Europe

British football clubs show a great reluctance to recognise the full seriousness of players' injuries: an unwillingness to accept that a key player is genuinely unfit to play. They almost seem to believe that by refusing to acknowledge the existence of an injury, they can make it go away. The result is that players turn out for matches in which they should not be playing at all.

Some clubs will do anything to get you to play. The pressures are very subtle but very real. The decision is always left to the players, of course, but it is very difficult to refuse when club officials are telling you that there is nothing to worry about. If you do have the courage to say no, they think you are shirking, that you don't want to play. You can be made to feel like a coward and become an outcast. I met this attitude throughout my career, from the time I was with Huddersfield Town to the eleven years I spent with Manchester United, and in my experience all clubs are guilty to some degree. I have played many times when I was not a hundred per cent fit, and I was certainly not the only one to do so. I have seen players go out who couldn't walk properly; but because they have had pain-killing injections, or pills, and are strapped up, they get through a match. After the game, though, they are in severe pain. I myself have played many times after having pain-killing injections in my knee or ankle. I have often spent forty-five minutes before a match with my knee under the cold water tap, and towards the end of my career I even used a cold water hose in an attempt to deaden pain. I have seen other players with their feet in buckets of ice.

Such are the lengths to which footballers are often forced to go to meet the demands of their clubs. They wouldn't send horses out to run the way they send players out. Ironically, there is no credit for doing it either, because if you aren't fit you can't really do yourself full justice, and in the long run no good is done for the player or the team. After the match, no one is going to start making excuses for you by saying 'yes, but the lad wasn't fit to play', because that begs the question 'why *did* he play?' The supporters see twenty-two players on the field:

they assume that all are fit, and judge them on their performance. Towards the end of my career I was being judged on performances that were really less than my best, but people didn't realise that because of my injuries I couldn't do it any more. I am convinced that the long term effect of playing in too many matches in which I should not have played shortened my career; it certainly kept me out of United's team which won the European Cup Final. If I had my time again, I just would not play in some of the matches in which I did play.

Things have undoubtedly improved a lot in recent years, but we still have a long way to go to catch up with the rest of Europe. Heaven knows, I found enough wrong with my life in Italy, but the one thing you could not fault the Italians for was their treatment of players. They had their priorities right. To them the players were the most important people in the club: they paid everyone else's wages, and accordingly they were treated like royalty. At Torino our medical unit was like a mini-hospital, with a doctor, three physio's and an impressive array of medical equipment. British clubs at that time were getting by with a box of plasters, a few bandages and the 'magic sponge'. It was a case of 'get out on to the track and try and do your best'. Once when I was injured in Italy I was sent to a spa village up in the Alps where the waters were supposed to have healing powers. I spent three days encased in mud up to my waist; it was unbelievable. I couldn't imagine that happening in Huddersfield.

The Italians realised that to perform well an athlete has to be in prime physical and mental condition. In Italy there would never be any pressure on a player to play if he wasn't fit. They would naturally hope that he would be fit, but if there was any doubt at all, then he didn't play. Perhaps having fewer fixtures and smaller playing staffs made it easier for them. In Turin we only had about twenty players – we didn't have reserve or youth teams. Through being looked after properly, players in Europe generally have a longer playing life than players in Britain. In Italy the supreme example of that at the moment is Gianni Rivera, who was playing when I was there and who is still going strong with AC Milan.

One thing I got used to in Italy and missed when I came back was a daily rub-down. Over there it was part of the routine, but in Britain it was considered a bit fay; not part and parcel of the way to treat players. The only time I got a rub-down with United was when we were involved in cup-ties and went to the Norbreck Hydro, at Blackpool, where they did have a couple of masseurs.

To be fair, I know that things have changed in recent years, and players are much better looked after than they were. United have one of the best set-ups, and Manchester City have a rehabilitation unit. I know that facilities at some of the bigger clubs, such as Liverpool, Everton, Arsenal and so on, have improved a great deal since I was playing, but most of the poorer clubs are still living in the dark ages, and there is a long way to go. It would be ludicrous to suggest that European teams never field an unfit player, because obviously they sometimes do; but in the main it does not happen. Certainly far fewer 'unfit' players appear on the continent than in Britain, although I think that the shortage of good players in British football is probably making clubs take more care of them now than they once did.

*   *   *   *   *

Back in 1967 I was having great difficulty convincing people at Old Trafford that there really was something wrong with my right knee. Some injuries are plainly visible, such as pulled muscles or swollen ankles, but with others there is nothing to see, and that is where the problem arises. I was suffering severe pains in my knee, particularly when I kicked the ball with my right instep, which was something I did most of the time. Rotating the leg to kick in this fashion has the effect of opening the knee joint, and that was where the trouble stemmed from. I would get sharp pains during a game, and then afterwards my knee would stiffen up and become extremely sore. Time and again I was asked to pin-point the exact source of the pain and then the needle would go in for yet another injection of cortizone. That was supposed to disperse the pain, but it never really worked. Our physiotherapist kept telling me that the problem was in my mind, something I was imagining. I used to ask him: 'If it's all in the mind, why don't I get the pain in my head?'

My troubles had started with the kick on the knee that I got when I was playing for Scotland against Poland in 1965. Since then it had got steadily worse, although the long rest I had in the summer of 1966 had given me some relief during the following season. However, in the summer of 1967 we had no break. We went on a long tour of Australia and America before running into the new season, which was when the problem reached its unhappy climax. During the 1967–68 season I played in only twenty-three league matches, many of them when I should not have played, and perhaps more significantly I scored only seven league goals. In the European Cup, I played in only three of our nine matches and scored twice. I had more treatment in six months than a player ought to have in an entire career, and I ended the season in a hospital bed watching on television as United won the European Cup.

Ironically the first time I experienced any trouble that season was at the end of August, after I had been playing golf at Chorlton. My knee swelled up as it filled with fluid. I loved playing golf, it was the one relaxation I had, but unfortunately it is a sport which puts some strain on your knees – particularly if you already have a knee problem, as I had. I could feel it beginning to stiffen up as I played my round, but I used to play on and hope that I wouldn't be too sore. In the end it became a hopeless struggle, and eventually, as much as I liked playing golf, I had to accept that I couldn't combine it with playing football. Something had to go, and there was only one solution – forget the golf. My clubs went into the attic, and from 1968 until I finished playing football in 1974 they only came out again during the summer.

After that first bout of trouble I missed three matches, but I was back in action by the middle of September, in time for the start of our European Cup campaign. Our first opponents were Hibernian of Malta. David Sadler and I scored a couple of goals apiece in the first leg at Old Trafford, where we won 4–0. That was generally felt to be a bad result against such weak opposition, and certainly the Maltese were delighted. The trip to Malta for the return leg was memorable in more ways than one. The scenes when we arrived at Luqa airport were unbelievable. Thousands of the local people were there to greet us and they all seemed to be Manchester United supporters. During our stay in Malta we were virtually imprisoned in the Phoenicia Hotel in Valetta, because whenever any of us went outside we were mobbed. They were Manchester United daft.

When we came to play the match, another surprise was in store. We had heard about Maltese pitches before we got there, but the Empire Stadium was still something to believe when we saw it. The playing surface was made up of compressed sand which was bumpy and uneven, rather like an unmade road. It was a good job we were starting with a four goal lead. Had it been only a couple, we might have been struggling. As it was we achieved a rather undignified goalless draw, which was ample to take us through to the next round of the competition. Needless to say, playing on that surface was no good for my knee – I was apprehensive when I first saw the pitch, and sure enough it just kept jarring the injury. After the match I was in quite a bit of pain.

Between the middle of September and the end of October I played in thirteen consecutive matches, including one for Scotland. It was my longest unbroken run of the season. Even then I played a number of times when I wasn't really up to it. Several times I ducked out of treatment because I was so sick of being on the table all the time. There were certain days when I knew that the training wasn't going to be particularly strenuous on my knee, so I would just train and swallow the pain. In the evenings I was putting hot Kaolin poultices on my leg. Kaolin was prescribed by the club, but I often used it off my own bat. At first I only used it when I was actually injured, but in the 1967–68 season I had Kaolin on my leg every night. That too was quite a painful process because the poultices are meant to be put on hot, and after a while my leg became very tender round the knee area. Another treatment I was using at home, which I had learned from Roy Goodall in my days at Huddersfield, was to run alternately very hot and ice cold water on my leg. This had a sort of flushing effect on the injury and did give a spot of relief. One way or another I turned our bathroom into something resembling a hospital casualty ward, and although I used plenty of bandages to keep the Kaolin from making a mess, some of it invariably ended up on the sheets. Although I doubt if I could have gone on playing without interruption for much longer, it was not actually the injury which ended the thirteen match sequence. That came about when I was suspended after being sent off during a league match against Arsenal.

Arsenal were a fairly hard side in those days. They were coached by Dave Sexton at the time and had adopted a system of very tight marking. From the beginning of the game it was obvious that Ian Ure was going to be marking me, in more ways than one. He was kicking me from one end of the park to the other. Naturally, I gave him a bit back but it really was a case of me committing one foul for every four of his. Eventually, of course, things had to boil over.

Whenever I got into trouble it always seemed to be as a result of retaliation. Over the years Matt Busby had had me in his office many times and asked me to try not to retaliate. I had been making a really conscious effort, and I thought that I had done quite well. Before the Arsenal match I had had only two bookings in the three years since my previous sending off. My record was looking remarkably good, but it was about to go up in smoke once again.

There were only eight minutes of the match remaining when Ian clattered me for the umpteenth time, and then gave me a kick as I was lying on the floor. It was the last straw. I had come to the end of my tether. I got up and took a wild swing at him which actually missed the target, but the referee, Mr George McCabe of Sheffield, turned round at the crucial moment – no doubt attracted by the shout which went up from the crowd – and saw my fist flying. He had already spoken to the pair of us earlier in the game, so I suppose it was inevitable that he would send us off. The incident undoubtedly looked bad, and yet once again it was the retaliation that had caught the eye. Although I do admit that I wasn't entirely innocent, Ian should really have been sent off earlier for some of his fouls on me and if he had been, then I wouldn't have been in trouble at all. Once again it was a case of a

117

referee giving a forward player inadequate protection. I felt that I was actually being sent off for nothing anyway, because my punch hadn't even found its mark, which was remarkable in itself when you consider the size of Ian's chin . . .

I felt that some of the press reports of that match were less than fair to me. Several people were referring to 'the Law/Ure incident' and blaming each of us as much as the other, which was ridiculous. He had been kicking me throughout the game and although I did retaliate, retaliation was my only crime. Some of the newspapers were speculating that we might get a three, or even a six month suspension, which was ludicrous, but because it was being suggested in the papers I began to think that it might happen. Other players were getting a week or a fortnight for being sent off, but whenever I was involved everyone seemed to expect a much tougher punishment, which was what invariably happened. When it was later announced that we had each got a six week ban, I was both relieved that it wasn't more and yet aggrieved because I still felt that I was being hard done by. Ian was the main offender and should have had a greater punishment than me.

By a strange coincidence, Ian and I shared the same bedroom a fortnight after our sending off, when Scotland were in Belfast for a match against Northern Ireland. That caused quite a lot of comment and speculation, but there was never any question of there being a problem between us. We had shared rooms many times before, and were actually quite good mates off the field. There was no ill feeling whatsoever. Players follow instructions and do things in the heat of the moment during a match, but after the game it's gone. Off the park it's a different ball game, as they say. There are exceptions, of course, but generally speaking there is no animosity between players off the field. Ian had set out to do a job on me exactly as I had done on Danny Blanchflower years earlier. When I threw the punch at him, I was disappointed at the time that it hadn't found its mark, because I was momentarily angry. But after the event when tempers had cooled, I was glad that I had missed him. We played in the same team in Ireland and were just as good mates then as we had ever been before.

During the match in Ireland, which we lost 1–0, I got another kick on my troublesome right knee, which was particularly ironic since the game was played almost exactly two years to the day after the match in which I had first been kicked on the same place, playing for Scotland against Poland.

I played in two league matches following that international before starting my suspension, but although a six week rest ought to have done my knee good, I was reporting for treatment again within a week. I was still in training of course, and the first sign of trouble came when

I had pain behind my knee after sprinting. Instead of enjoying a rest period, I seemed to spend more time having treatment while I was suspended than I had at any previous stage of the season. I had more of the inevitable cortizone injections and in mid-December my consultant, Mr Glass, said in a letter to the club that he thought the best way to treat my injury was by 'masterly inactivity . . . let him play . . . I think that the condition will probably resolve itself'. Unfortunately that assessment proved to be wrong, and although I did play in a sequence of seven consecutive matches immediately following my suspension, by early January I was in an even worse state than ever.

On 11 January 1968, after examining me yet again, Mr Glass offered the suggestion that there might be a piece of cartilage left in my knee from the operation which I had had while I was with Huddersfield Town nine years earlier. He suggested that I should continue playing, but train only on soft ground, and undergo an operation to remove the 'posterior horn of cartilage' during the coming close season. I couldn't believe it. As far as I was concerned I had had my cartilage removed, and the idea that a piece left behind was the cause of the trouble seemed ridiculous.

Throughout that month I continued playing, but I was always in pain. On 27 January we drew 2–2 with Spurs at Old Trafford in the third round of the FA Cup, and after that match Matt Busby decided that while we were in London for the replay I should take the opportunity to visit a Harley Street specialist. United lost the replay 1–0. That was the match in which David Herd made his comeback, but I didn't play and while the rest of the team were preparing for it I was visiting Mr Osmond-Clarke, an orthopaedic surgeon, who later on treated the Queen and eventually received a knighthood. His report, which I did not personally see until years later, offered a startling opinion, which in time was to prove correct. After outlining the medical history connected with the knee, Mr Osmond-Clarke reported that: 'The behaviour of this knee . . . is a powerful indictment of its competence to stand up to first-class professional football . . . especially in the years since late 1965. There may indeed be a tag of the external semilunar cartilage still in the joint and it might help to remove it . . . *But the fact will remain that this is a degenerating joint and that nothing and nobody can prevent further deterioration, be it slow or fast. My own view is that this knee has reached a stage when it will handicap Mr Law in top-flight play and I very much doubt if it will stand up to it for more than another season or two.* Even then I would suspect that the knee would give rise to many complaints and periods of unfitness . . . My conclusion is that if Mr Law and the club are agreeable to take a chance on a further exploration of the knee prolonging the life of the knee in first-class professional Association Football, I feel it would be reasonable to take that chance, *but I cannot confess to be optimistic myself about the possibilities of a successful outcome . . .'*

Just over a week after I had seen Mr Osmond-Clarke, a meeting was held at Old Trafford between Mr Glass, Matt Busby, Dr McHugh and Ted Dalton, at which it was decided that for a four week period I should continue full training while having Faradism treatment and taking aspirin tablets prescribed by Dr McHugh. After four weeks the position would be reviewed.

During that period I managed to play in two league matches but I was still having severe pain and receiving cortizone injections. During my suspension United had progressed to the third round of the European Cup by beating the Jugoslav side, Sarajevo, in the second round.

The first of our two matches against Gornik Zabrze of Poland was due to be played at Old Trafford on 28 February. The day before the match I experienced excruciating pain in the knee while I was training. The following morning – the day of the match – I went to see Mr Glass at the Jewish Hospital to have another pain-killing injection. This time he used Protocain, which was a drug I hadn't previously been given. After the injection I went home to get a couple of hours sleep before meeting the rest of the team at 4.30pm. Because I was due to be playing that evening, my wife, Di, had taken the kids to her sister's and was not due home until late that evening, so I was in the house alone.

It turned out that I was allergic to Protocain, and while I was in bed my leg came up like a barrage balloon. I woke up in a state of agonised delirium. I couldn't possibly walk, but with no one else in the house it was up to me to telephone the club to tell them what had happened. I had to crawl head-first down the stairs to get to the telephone in the hall. Somehow in my fevered condition I managed it. The following day I was admitted to St Joseph's Hospital, Whalley Range, where Mr Glass drained the fluid from my knee which was an experience I can only liken to having a large stone block lifted off my head. I was in agony; my leg was bursting, and I could feel the growing relief as the syringe did its work. I don't know how much fluid came out of my knee, but it seemed like a bucketful. After it was over I was put into a splint and felt as if I was in heaven. (On a point of interest, United beat Gornik 2–0 and later lost the second leg 1–0 in Poland, to progress to the European Cup semi-final for the fourth time in four attempts.)

February had been a month of pain and trouble, and March was to be little better. I came out of hospital after five days in time to say goodbye to my wife, who was off to Scotland to await the arrival of our third child. I spent a very miserable few weeks living alone at home and travelling each day to the ground for treatment. I played in only one match, towards the end of the month, when we were beaten 3–1 at home by Manchester City. At one stage of the season United had led the first divison league table by five points, but a succession of bad results, including three defeats at home, frittered that lead away and it was City who were coming through to snatch the championship from our grasp in the final weeks of the season. To be honest though, my thoughts were not really on championships at that time. I was so fed up with being continually injured that I decided to take steps of my own to try to cure the problem.

I had a friend named Paddy McGrath who was having trouble with a bad back. He used to visit an osteopath for treatment and always came back feeling very much better. I must say that up to that time I had always thought of osteopaths as being some sort of quacks, but by now I was prepared to try anything – and when Paddy suggested that I should see his Mr Millwood, I was delighted to do so. I went to see him without the club's knowledge, and it was a while before they found out.

They were not very pleased when they did, and there was quite a row, but I said: 'It's my life, and my leg, and I'll do it my way.' I had tried all the routine methods provided by the club, now I wanted to try something of my own.

Mr Millwood used to manipulate my joints, which had the effect of relaxing the stiffness. I really felt that it was doing me good. After every game, though, the knee would stiffen up again, and I would have to return for more treatment. I came to be very dependent on Mr Millwood and actually went on seeing him for the rest of my playing days. Originally of course I had gone to see him about my knee, but eventually I was visiting him with other injuries too, and in fact over the next six years I spent a great deal of time in his surgery. Once, when I first started seeing him, he told me that I shouldn't train so I pretended to have 'flu and took a week off. Whatever the pros and cons of the various treatments I was getting, there was no doubt that rest was above all the one thing which invariably made me feel better.

I played my last five matches of the season in April. My son, Robert, was born on the 14 April, so my family were still in Scotland when we came to meet Real Madrid in the European Cup semi-final ten days later. By this time Mr Millwood had started to strap my knee up in an effort to hold the joint together, which was when the club found out about my private treatment. I turned up for the match with my knee heavily bandaged. It was solid, like a ballbearing race with no movement. I hadn't done a great deal of training and I wasn't feeling particularly good. I certainly wasn't properly fit and I shouldn't have played. The season was nearly over though, and I was still thinking

121

that if I could get through the odd game I would be all right. It was a terrible game. I was told to stay up front and I did virtually nothing. We won 1–0 with a goal scored by George Best, but it was not a particularly good result. This was not the Real Madrid of old, and if we had been at our best we would have slaughtered them. They were a poor side compared to what they had been, but even so one goal was a slender lead to be taking to Madrid for the return leg.

Five days after that match my season came to an end. We played West Brom at the Hawthorns in a match which should have presented us with two championship points. West Brom were through to the FA Cup Final, and they were in a safe position in the league. Normally teams in that position were a soft touch in league matches in the weeks before their appearance at Wembley, but it was one of those days when everything went in for them and, after I had missed a sitter early in the match, they beat us 6–3 and our title hopes took another set-back. I was back on the treatment table again after the match, and at the beginning of May I decided to ask for yet another medical opinion about my knee. The following day the club sent me to see a Manchester specialist who, after examining me, gave me yet another cortizone injection but could offer no new suggestion about the cause of my trouble.

A few days later we flew to Madrid for the second leg of the European Cup semi-final. We had been there before of course, but even so it was still a shock to be reminded again of the fabulous facilities that some of the top European clubs have for their players. The Bernabeu Stadium really is magnificent. Players have individual baths, showers and changing rooms. Everything is top class. British players get embarrassed when they see that, and then realise that the foreign team has to visit our grounds and use our shabby facilities. Here again, I know that improvements have been made in recent years, but not anywhere near sufficiently. Even Wembley, the national stadium, is a barn compared to the best facilities on the continent. I remember being very disappointed when I first went there to find that the dressing room had three baths and a few showers. This was supposed to be the Mecca of British football but it was a poor contrast to what I had seen in Italy. We still have a long way to go, and it doesn't only apply to players' facilities – the public deserves better too. I believe that the government should make money available for improving grounds, because after all they take enough out of the game one way and another. We live in an age of leisure, where people have many alternative forms of entertainment and they won't suffer to watch football in discomfort. A new stadium is being built at Hampden Park, and I only hope that it is up to scratch. Real Madrid's Bernabeu Stadium is more than thirty years old, which is food for thought.

When we arrived in Spain, it was still intended that I should play in the match, but I had a fitness test on the morning of the game and decided that it was hopeless. I clearly wasn't fit and the match was far too important for the club to start taking chances. Had I played that night, I would probably have played in the European Cup Final. The choice was mine, but after the lads had put up such a tremendous performance in Madrid, coming back from 3–1 down at half-time to draw 3–3, I didn't think it would be fair on the players who had played if I came back just for the Final. I knew I wasn't fit, and they knew I wasn't fit, and there was far too much at stake for the club.

By now it had been decided that I should have an exploratory operation on my knee. Until they actually open you up, these things are all rather hit and miss. Players sometimes respond to one form of treatment or another, and then an operation may not be necessary. In my case we had exhausted all the possibilities we could think of, and I still had the problem, which meant that an operation was really all that was left. Matt Busby asked me what I wanted to do. He suggested that I should go to London with the team and watch the European Cup Final, then have the operation afterwards. I didn't fancy that. I said that I preferred to have the operation as quickly as possible, then concentrate on getting fit again. So three days before the Final I was admitted to St Joseph's Hospital, where Mr Glass opened up my knee and took out a piece of cartilage between an inch and an inch and a half long. I still have it at home in a jar. Before he set off for Wembley, Matt Busby came to see me in hospital and I said to him: 'At least I'm glad of one thing. There was something there. Now I've proved that it wasn't just in my mind.'

Missing the European Cup Final was obviously one of the greatest disappointments of my career, but at least it was something I had been able to anticipate. Had I been injured a week before the game, I would have been utterly depressed, but I had known for some time that I was probably going to miss it. Even so, it was a rather melancholy experience sitting in hospital watching the match on television, and not until the following day did it really sink in that this was the greatest thing that had ever happened to the club. Ten years after the disaster of Munich, Matt Busby had guided his team to the greatest honour in club football.

As for me, I came out of hospital and started back on the road to recovery. My medical record charted my progress, showing the improvement with comments like 'very good' and 'excellent' until on the 11 July, Mr Glass declared me 'fit to do full training'. It sounded rather like the end of a fairy story, but the truth was that whatever had been done to my knee, and whatever had been found inside it, I was not cured. I was still destined to be plagued with knee trouble for the rest of my playing days. I did my best, and sometimes it would be all right, but never for long, and most of the time I was playing in severe pain. I've always believed that it was my visits to the osteopath which kept me going and enabled me to play for a further six years, but there is no doubt that Mr Osmond-Clarke had it right when he said of my knee, 'This is a degenerating joint and nothing and nobody can prevent further deterioration'.

CHAPTER 11

Sir Matt Stands Down

Matt Busby was awarded his knighthood in the Queen's Birthday Honours List six weeks after United had become the first English club to win the European Cup. It was a recognition of his magnificent twenty-three-year reign as manager of Manchester United during which he had kept the club at the top of English football, built three great sides, and despite the tragedy of Munich, seen them win five league championships, the FA Cup twice, and now the greatest prize of all, the European Cup. United themselves were on the crest of a wave, and yet ironically even in the moment of triumph there were already voices raised saying that the team was over the hill, and that the time had come for Matt to hand over to a younger man. The 1968–69 season was indeed to be the last in which we would have Matt at the helm, and events during the season tended to both prove and disprove the criticisms of the team. Our league form was not good and suggested that the critics might be right; but on the other hand we came within an ace of reaching the European Cup Final for a second time. I believe that we were robbed of that opportunity and that had we not been we would have retained Europe's top prize. Who then was right?

One of our earliest experiences that season was to visit Argentina for the first of two matches against Estudiantes to decide the World Club Championship. They were the champions of South America; we the champions of Europe. The competition, now defunct, had seemed like a good idea when it was first conceived in 1960, but it had an unfortunate history of trouble. Celtic had met that in the previous year, when their matches against Racing Club degenerated into brawls and Jock Stein had said that his team would never again play in the competition, should they ever again win the European Cup.

Because of Celtic's experience doubts had been expressed at Old Trafford about the wisdom of our going to South America, but arrangements had been made and Matt Busby decided that, despite his reservations, perhaps we had better see it through. We flew from

England on the evening of Saturday, 21 September 1968, after beating Newcastle United 3–1 in a league match at Old Trafford that afternoon. It was a hell of a trip which took the best part of a day, and because of the five hour time difference at the other end, it took a couple of days for us to acclimatise once we had arrived.

We had been warned that we could expect a hostile reception, but even so we were amazed at how bad it was when we got there. Two years previously, Alf Ramsey had called the Argentine football team 'animals' after their World Cup quarter-final tie against England at Wembley: people were still talking about that when I went to Buenos Aires for the World Cup Finals in 1978. In 1968 the comment was very much in their minds, and we were the first English team to visit Argentina since Ramsey's outburst. Actually I have always thought that had Rattin not been sent off at Wembley, England would not have beaten Argentina; however, that is another matter. When we arrived in Buenos Aires in 1968 all the pent-up hostility of the Argentine nation was waiting for us. The most obvious target was Nobby Stiles, who had rather undeservedly earned a reputation for being a bit of a hard man. The Argentine press labelled him '*El Assassin*', and things were not helped by an article in the match programme written by the Benfica manager, Otto Gloria, in which he described Nobby as 'brutal, bad intentioned, and a bad sportsman'.

It seemed that everything which could be done to upset us and create a bad atmosphere was done. On the eve of the match we were invited to a reception in Buenos Aires where we were supposed to meet the Estudiantes team. We were staying at the famous Hindu Club, the same headquarters chosen by the Italians in 1978, which is a good hour and a half drive out of Buenos Aires. We had already done our fair share of travelling to get to Argentina but, never one to turn down a chance to improve public relations, Matt Busby accepted the offer and we duly turned up at the reception. There was no sign of Estudiantes, but we were told that they had been held up in a traffic jam and we settled down to wait. Almost two hours later we were still waiting, by which time it was obvious that they were not coming. Matt was furious, but there was nothing we could do except return to the Hindu Club and go to bed.

We hadn't met the Estudiantes players, but they were supposed to be students – which is what the name means – so we didn't really anticipate too much trouble in the match, which was played in the Boca Juniors Stadium. How wrong can you be? It was frightening; far worse than anything I had experienced in Italy, and worse than anything I have experienced anywhere else, either before or since. They were spitting, kicking and punching, and after they had knocked you down they would 'help' you to your feet. That looked fine from a spectator's point of view, but what the spectator couldn't see was that the man helping you to your feet was actually pinching you under the armpits. The man marking me was supposed to be a student dentist. He had a sweat band round his head and looked more like an Apache. As he lunged at me with his eyes narrowed in a warlike frenzy, all that was missing was the tomahawk. For the only time in my life I was in agreement with Alf Ramsey; these players *were* animals. It was impossible to play football and we didn't try very hard. Survival was the name of that game. One of them butted Nobby Stiles, cutting Nobby's head in the process, then dropped to the ground as if shot, giving the impression that the offence had been committed the other way round. At first I thought that the referee was going to send Nobby off, but when he saw the cut over Nobby's eye he obviously thought better of it. Ten minutes later the linesman allowed Estudiantes to play on when they were clearly offside. Nobby lost his patience and gave the official a V-sign . . . and this time he *was* off. The opposition were getting away with murder and we had a man sent off for making a gesture. It was obvious that whatever happened we were going to be adjudged the sinners. We lost the match 1–0, but were glad to be going back home without too much damage to life and limb. Bobby Charlton had taken a terrible kick on his shin, but apart from that everyone seemed to be in one piece.

We felt that we might extract some revenge in the return match, three weeks later, but it was not to be. A defensive error gave them an early goal and after that things never went right. Midway through the first half, I was carried off with a gashed shin after their goalkeeper had come at me with his foot out and gone down the front of my right leg with his aluminium studs. In the second half George Best was sent off, together with Estudiantes' Medina after a scuffle, and although Willie Morgan pulled a goal back late in the game and Brian Kidd had the ball in the net seconds after the final whistle, we lost the tie on aggregate 2–1. It had been a bad experience and one which we vowed would never be repeated should we win the European Cup again. In fact we were not the last to have trouble playing in the World Club Championship. The following season AC Milan were caught up in it, and three years later Ajax had their share.

The question of whether or not we would agree to play in the World Club Championship was academic until such time as we had won the European Cup again, and I believe that we should have retained it in 1969. We had an easy passage through the first round, where we met the Southern Irish club, Waterford. We beat them 3–1 in Dublin, and ?–1 at Old Trafford. This tie produced an unusual scoring record for

Denis Law

me because, despite missing a penalty in Dublin, I scored a hat-trick in both matches, with three goals in the first and four in the second. We were without George Best, the 1968 European Footballer of the Year, who was suspended when we met Anderlecht in the first leg of the second round at Old Trafford. Again I missed a penalty, but still scored two of the goals in our 3–0 victory, which took me to a new club record of fourteen goals in the European Cup, nine of them scored that season. The record had previously been held by Dennis Viollet, with thirteen. In 1956, United's pre-Munich team had beaten Anderlecht 10–0 in a European Cup tie, but the team which we met in the 1968–69 season was a vastly different proposition. By now Dutch and Belgian football had begun to make great strides and we needed the early goal which Carlo Sartori scored in the second leg in Belgium to make it 4–0 on aggregate. After that, Anderlecht put us under tremendous pressure and scored three times, to come within one goal of taking the match to a replay. In the end we were a shade fortunate to get away with it. Our quarter-final opponents were Rapid Vienna whom we beat 3–0 in the first leg at Old Trafford. I missed the return match in Vienna, through injury, but the team put up a great performance to earn a goalless draw and a place in the semi-final. It was the fifth time that United had reached the European Cup semi-finals in as many attempts, and our opponents were to be the Italian champions, AC Milan.

The San Siro stadium is one of the most daunting places in the world for any away team, particularly in a European tournament match, and to this day no British team has won there. Realistically the best you can hope for is a draw or a narrow defeat. During the match Nobby Stiles had to be carried off with his knee 'locked' and, although we put up a reasonable performance, goals by Hamrin and Sormani, scored either side of half-time, gave them a 2–0 victory and left us with a great deal to do in the second leg at Old Trafford. The way the Italians pack their defences away from home makes it very difficult to score goals against them. They are the world masters of negative play and it is very difficult to find a way through their crowded penalty areas. There is also the problem of their over-physical approach to the game, and it has always amazed me the way referees let them get away with it. It is as though they accept that that is the Italians' normal way of playing, and let them get on with it. The hacking and tripping which characterise Italian football seem to be frequently ignored when the Italians are doing it, but let a British player commit the same foul and he is soon sent off.

Actually, in the second leg against Milan I *did* get away with a spot of mayhem myself. I was being marked by my old Torino club mate,

128

Roberto Rosato, who by now had become an Italian international. Roberto and I were great mates in Turin, but now we were playing football and he had clearly been given instructions to do a job on me. He didn't seem to care whether or not he kicked the ball, so long as he made sure that I didn't. It was the familiar old story of me getting whacked time and time again. Several times I warned Roberto in my pidgin Italian to stop it, but of course he took no notice and in the end I had to wait until the referee wasn't looking and extract my own retribution. Unfortunately mine was not the only violent act that night and the Milan goalkeeper, Cudicini, was knocked out by a missile thrown by some lout at the Stretford End.

There has always been a certain amount of suspicion over the years that some match officials have been 'got at' in important matches involving top Italian teams. It is something which is obviously very difficult to prove, but nevertheless Brian Glanville of the *Sunday Times* wrote an interesting feature on the subject a year or two ago. Quite recently, and not for the first time, AC Milan have been in trouble with UEFA for offering illegal gifts to referees and linesmen. I suppose it is inevitable therefore that whenever there is a controversial decision involving an Italian team, which goes in their favour, there will be those who wonder whether or not it was just one of those things, or whether it might have been something more sinister. I offer no opinion other than that AC Milan had a diabolical decision given in their favour at Old Trafford which robbed us of an equalising goal and ended our involvement in the European Cup. It took us until the seventieth minute of the match finally to break down their defence, when Bobby Charlton pulled back one of the two goals by which we were trailing from the first leg. We then mounted tremendous pressure in going for the equaliser, and seven minutes later we seemed to have scored it. There was a scramble in the Milan penalty area and after a couple of rebounds I stabbed the ball in the direction of their goal. It was rolling quite slowly, but had clearly travelled at least a foot over the line when a Milan defender slid into the net and hooked it back into play. The French referee was within a few yards of the incident, and yet to my utter amazement he waved play on. He had one of the best views of what happened of anyone in the ground, and yet he seemed to be the only person there who didn't think it was a goal. Willie Morgan had been following up and could have finished it off, but just as Roger Hunt had done with Geoff Hurst's goal off the crossbar for England against West Germany, in the World Cup Final, he left it because he knew that it had already crossed the line. Practically everyone in the ground knew that it was a goal, and television and photographic evidence later proved to my complete satisfaction that it was, but it still didn't count. With that travesty of justice United were out of the European Cup. Had that goal counted I believe that we could have gone on to win the tie that night. In any event a draw would have given us a replay in Brussels which I think we would have won. Had we done so, our final opponents would have been Ajax, who were not yet the force which they later became. AC Milan beat them 4–1 to win the European Cup and I am certain that, had we reached the Final, United could have done just as well. So, in a sense, a single controversial disallowed goal cost us our European crown.

What was particularly disappointing about that result was that it was regarded by a lot of people, and a large section of the press, as a sign that United were finished. We had failed at the semi-final stage of the European Cup by a single goal and yet the talk the following day was of us being over the top, of it being time for us to rebuild. Had my goal counted, and had we gone on to retain the European Cup, then presumably we would still have been regarded as the best team in Europe. Because that hadn't happened, really by the margin of a single goal, we were being written off. To me this was crazy, and yet it was typical of the unrealistic attitude of a lot of people in and around British football. One goal either way can be the making or breaking of a team. Perhaps in our case we were being judged against our successful record over the previous six seasons, during which we had been continually battling for honours and had won the FA Cup, two League Championships and the European Cup. Even if that were true, to write us off after a season in which we had reached the semi-final of the European Cup and the sixth round of the FA Cup, where we were beaten 1–0 by Everton, was at the very least harsh.

To be fair to the critics, our league form in the 1968–69 season was not good. In March we had been sixth from the bottom of the table, but had rallied to finish eleventh. That was a poor show for the European Champions, but to put things into perspective it should be remembered that, in addition to our commitment to trying to retain the European Cup, it had been a dreadful year for injuries and we had hardly had a settled side all season. I missed a dozen league matches myself, but apart from me we had lost Johnny Aston with a broken leg in August, which was when Matt Busby bought Willie Morgan; Bobby Charlton had been out for nine weeks with knee ligament trouble; Nobby Stiles and Francis Burns were both having cartilage problems – Francis actually had two spells in hospital having cartilages removed during that season; Tony Dunne suffered a broken jaw; and on top of that we had the usual crop of one hundred and one other routine injuries which any team suffers in a season. There, to me, was ample explanation of our poor league form, and our performances in the

European Cup ought to have been sufficient proof to the doubters that we were far from over the hill. Several of us were in our late twenties, but that is an age when a lot of players are reaching their prime. The exception was Bill Foulkes, who was then aged 37 and may just have been losing a yard of pace. We felt that perhaps we did need a new centre-half, which is a key position in any team. We had started to concede one or two goals and Matt Busby had looked unsuccessfully for a replacement, but to suggest that because of that the whole of the team was finished, was ludicrous.

From my point of view, it had been a season of mixed fortune. I was still having problems with my knee, but the fourteen league goals I scored proved that I was in better shape than I had been the previous year. I had also notched nine in the European Cup, and the seven I scored in five FA Cup ties made me the club's leading scorer in all competitions that season, and took me six clear of Jack Rowley's record of twenty-eight FA Cup goals for the club. Unfortunately, though, the cumulative effect of too many matches was again beginning to catch up with me, and after another close-season tour I was destined to face yet another season of treatment; and by then I would be playing for a new boss.

Matt Busby announced his intention to step down from the manager's job in January 1969. He had been unwell for some time and was having problems with his back. He felt that the job of running Manchester United had become too much for one man and that the time had come to hand on to a younger person. In April it was announced that our reserve team manager, Wilf McGuinness, had been appointed chief coach. The idea was that Sir Matt was to become general manager, dealing with all of the club's massive volume of public relations work, and that from the start of the 1969–70 season, Wilf would be running the team.

CHAPTER 12

Transfer Listed Again

In a way, the decision to put Wilf McGuinness in charge of the team marked United's acceptance of the new, methodical style of play which had become fashionable in Britain since England had won the World Cup in 1966. In the years since then, we at Old Trafford had adopted a rather loose variation on the 4–2–4 and 4–3–3 themes, the latter being particularly useful when we were playing away legs of European matches, but our overall approach to the game under Matt Busby had still been based on attacking rather than defensive philosophy. The 4–2–4 formation simply meant that we had two wingers dropping back to help in midfield, and under either system the middle and front men would combine to give us six attackers at any time. Essentially our play was still based on the ability of individuals to do their own thing within the scope of a broad tactical approach.

In the game generally, though, since 1966 coaches had become the important figures. Wilf, who had been a member of Alf Ramsey's World Cup coaching staff, represented this 'brave new world' of football. It has been suggested that he failed because some of the senior players would not play for him. That allegation is completely untrue. The job of managing Manchester United is an enormous one at any time, and following Matt Busby was going to be a daunting task for anybody. Wilf was not the only one who found the task too great, and in my opinion he was not ready for the responsibility at the time he undertook it. I believe that the real reason he failed was that he tried to introduce an approach to the game which was totally alien to the players who had earned United their years of success. Having said that, it has to be remembered that we did reach three semi-finals under Wilf McGuinness, although the team was fifth from the bottom of the first division when he was relieved of his duties twenty months after taking over.

Following in Matt's footsteps, I suppose Wilf felt that he had to stamp his authority on things at an early stage. People were saying that he wasn't 'big' enough to handle big name players. The method he chose to prove that he was rocked the football world: he dropped me, and he dropped Bobby Charlton! The team had started the season badly. After drawing our opening fixture, away to Crystal Palace, we lost our first two home matches against Everton and Southamption, the latter by 4–1: all four Southampton goals were scored by their Welsh international centre-forward, Ron Davies, with his head. If you were looking for someone to blame in such circumstances, I suppose you would look to the centre-half, and possibly the goalkeeper, and in fact Bill Foulkes and Jimmy Rimmer were two of five players dropped for our next game, a midweek league match away to Everton. That was virtually the end of Bill's playing career; later that month Wilf paid out £80,000 to bring Ian Ure from Arsenal and soon after that Bill retired and took up a job coaching our youth players. Shay Brennan was also dropped for the match at Everton, but the real sensation was that Bobby Charlton and I were left out. The five players who came into the team were Alex Stepney, John Fitzpatrick, Paul Edwards, Don Givens and John Aston.

That was the first time in my career that I had been dropped. I believe that Bobby was particularly upset by it. For my part, I was stunned, but the silly thing was I felt certain that it was merely a gesture and that we would be back in the team by Saturday. The gesture may have impressed the public – I don't know about that – but it failed to impress anyone at Old Trafford. United lost the match at Everton 3–0, and sure enough when we drew 0–0 with Wolves at Molineux on the following Saturday, Law and Charlton were back in the team. That was the match in which Ian Ure made his debut, but for me it was the start of another depressing injury saga. I strained my groin and was out of the side for the next twelve matches.

One of the most significant changes brought about by Wilf, was his use of blackboard coaching at team talks. Matt Busby had used the blackboard only occasionally, to make a particular point, or perhaps to get us back to basics after a run of bad results; otherwise we hardly ever saw it. Wilf had it out all the time. Soon, every Friday, and sometimes on Saturday mornings too, we would have a session with the magnetic men and everyone in the team was given a set of instructions. Things became very complicated, with everyone expected to go out and play according to the blackboard. Instead of going out to play football, as they had been accustomed to doing, players were going out with their minds stuffed with plans and tactics. United had never played football that way and the effect was to cause confusion. Whereas Matt had laid down a broad simple philosophy for the game, on the basis that we were all intelligent players and knew what we should be doing within the context of the overall tactical plan, Wilf was trying to lay down a complete battle plan in advance.

In relation to United, and the players Wilf had at his disposal, this approach was rather naive. Hand in hand with it, our general attitude to the game was being changed from an attacking one to a defensive one, which meant that certain key players were no longer fashionable. In particular, Pat Crerand did not fit into Wilf's new style of play. Pat's greatest strength had always been his creative attacking flair. The one weak aspect of his game was his defensive skill. Accordingly Pat soon found himself out of favour. Willie Morgan, too, was a luxury that Wilf's style of play could do without. There was no place in a defence-orientated 4–3–3 for an old-fashioned attacking winger. Gradually the shape of the team changed as more defensive-minded players were brought in, many of them lads like Francis Burns, John Fitzpatrick, Steve James, Tony Young, Frank Kopel, and others who had served under Wilf in the youth and reserve teams. Although injury kept me out of action for most of the season anyway, I too eventually found myself sitting on the subs' bench. In the early days, one of the main features of my game had been my total involvement. Now, the problem of my constantly nagging injury meant that I couldn't cover the same amount of ground. I was having to conserve my energy and rely more on experience to get me through, which of course did not suit a system where work-rate was considered to be the greatest of all the virtues. My place in the side was taken by the young Italian boy, Carlo Sartori.

As we finished eighth in the league, in spite of our poor start, and reached two semi-finals, Wilf's first full season in the chair was seen as a reasonable success. He was formally appointed team manager before the start of the next season. The first of our semi-finals had been against Manchester City, in the League Cup in December. Three weeks previously City had beaten United 4–0 in a league match at Maine Road, and while the semi-final first leg was much closer, they again won, 2–1, after scoring from a disputed penalty in the last minute of the match. As the teams were leaving the field, George Best knocked the ball out of referee Jack Taylor's hand, for which he was later suspended for one month. I missed that match, but was recalled for the second leg, at Old Trafford, where I scored an early goal to cancel out City's lead. A key moment of the match was when they were awarded an indirect free-kick on the edge of our penalty area. Alex Stepney 'saved' Francis Lee's kick, but could only parry the ball to Mike Summerbee who slotted it home. Ironically, had Alex let the free kick go straight into the net it would not have counted, since the kick was 'indirect'. It would have been a dead ball. Instead it was a goal, and the eventual outcome of the match was a 2–2 draw, which meant that City were through to the League Cup Final, where they beat West Bromwich

Albion 2–1 to win the trophy.

A month later we had our revenge when we beat City 3–0 at Old Trafford in the fourth round of the FA Cup, en route to our second semi-final of the season. In the third round we had beaten Ipswich 1–0 at Portman Road, and after beating City we were drawn away to Northampton in the fifth. That match was George Best's first after his suspension, and he celebrated his return in style with six goals in our 8–2 victory.

In the sixth round we beat Middlesbrough 2–1 after a replay, which brought us face to face once again with our bogey team, Leeds United, in the semi-final. I was still in and out of the side, mainly through injury, and missed the first meeting at Hillsborough in March, which ended in the almost inevitable goalless draw. In the replay at Villa Park I was named as substitute, and came on in extra time in place of Carlo Sartori. I think that was possibly the last straw for Wilf as far as I was concerned. Within a minute of being on the field, I missed an open goal. The ball came across from the wing and I headed it wide from close range. Had the chance come a few minutes later, I am certain that I would have scored; however, that was practically my first touch of the ball and I hadn't had time to adjust to the pace of the game.

Once again the match ended nil-nil, and went to a second replay at Burnden Park, where we lost to a single goal scored by Billy Bremner. Towards the end of that match I was booked, as frustration began to get the better of us. Somehow that seemed to symbolise the wretched year I had had. I had struggled all season with injury, played in only ten league matches, and scored only twice. Things had reached a pretty desperate state. Even so, I was not prepared for the shock I received in April, when the retained list was published and I learned that I had been transfer-listed at £60,000. Also on the list was Shay Brennan, who played his last match for us against Spurs on 13 April, when he played outside-right and scored one of his rare goals. For me it was make or break time. People had begun to write me off and, although I didn't want to leave Old Trafford, there were no offers to buy me. The feeling was that I was finished. I knew it was being said that I couldn't do it any more, and I decided it was time to do something about that.

Because the 1970 World Cup Finals were due to take place in Mexico that summer, the league season had ended early. As I was on the transfer list I did not go on United's close-season tour of America. Once again, exactly as I had done in 1966, I found myself facing more than three months of free time. I decided to use it to get myself back to complete fitness before the start of the next season. Apart from a fortnight off around the time that my fourth son, Iain, was born on 5 May, I trained six days a week throughout that summer. I trained three days a week at the club, and three days a week at a private gym, where I did weight training in an effort to build up my leg muscles. By the time the 1970–71 season began, I was as near to one hundred per cent fitness as I felt I could be and the transfer matter had died a natural death.

Wilf was promoted from chief coach to team manager before the start of the 1970–71 season, but no one realised at the time that he had only four months left in the job. We started the season badly, taking only one point from our first three matches, and although we did then manage to string a couple of wins together, things were never really going well and matters reached a head during a disastrous twelve days in December.

The period began when we were beaten 4–1 at home in a league match by Manchester City. That was on 12 December. We had not won a league match at Old Trafford since beating West Brom 2–1 on 24 October. If our league form was poor, the saving grace was that after victories over Aldershot, Portsmouth, Chelsea and Crystal Palace, we had again reached the semi-final of the League Cup. As our semi-final opponents were third division Aston Villa, there at least seemed a reasonable prospect that we would be going to Wembley. Four days after our defeat by Manchester City, Villa held us to a 1–1 draw in the semi-final first leg at Old Trafford. On the Saturday we again crashed at home in the league, this time by 3–1 to Arsenal. Then, on 23 December, came the final indignity when we were beaten 2–1 in the League Cup semi-final second leg, at Villa Park. Brian Kidd actually gave us the lead after a quarter of an hour, but goals by Andy Lochhead and Pat McMahon saw us out of the competition, and virtually put Wilf McGuinness out of a job. On Boxing Day we were away to Derby County, where we earned a respectable 4–4 draw, but the match was Wilf's last as manager. Three days later it was announced from Old Trafford that he had been relieved of his duties and that Sir Matt would be resuming charge of the team until the end of the season.

The change of leadership had an almost immediate effect on morale. There was no question of anyone trying harder for Matt than they had done for Wilf, as has often been suggested. Simply, a change of attitude took place. United had always been a happy club, but under Wilf this had been progressively less and less the case. We had reached the stage where everything seemed to be crumbling and club spirit had reached rock bottom. I believe that this was largely due to the way we were being asked to play. Bad methods had led to bad results, which in turn led to a loss of morale. All that Matt did was to throw the blackboard out of the window and get players' minds free of defensive planning. He simply said, 'Let's get back to enjoying our football: let's go out and play', and that's what we did.

Naturally, he made a few team changes, too, and in due course most of the old faces were back in the side. We were in eighteenth place in the league when he took over, and by the end of the season we were eighth. Had we played like that all season, we would have been close to winning the championship, which seemed like a fair answer to those people who had been saying a year earlier that the team was finished.

Of course, it was not all plain-sailing after Matt had resumed control. His first match as manager was against Middlesbrough in the third round of the FA Cup and, after a 1–1 draw at Old Trafford, we lost the replay 2–1 on a snowbound pitch at Ayresome Park. Matt's first league match though was at Chelsea, where we won 2–1 to record only our third away win of the season in the league. It was a day notable for two things – first for a magnificent goal by Alan Gowling, who ran half of the length of the pitch to score it, and secondly for the absence of George Best, who failed to turn up to meet the rest of the team for the rail journey to London on the Friday. George had already been in trouble with the club during the previous week or so for failing to turn up for training on Christmas Day, and for arriving late for an FA disciplinary hearing in London at the beginning of January. This time Matt ran out of patience and sent for John Aston to take George's place in the match at Stamford Bridge. That was the start of a two-year chapter of events which eventually led to George quitting the game.

The victory over Chelsea began a run in which we took nine points from five games. On 6 February, the thirteenth anniversary of Munich, we beat Spurs 2–1 at Old Trafford, to record our first league victory at home for an incredible three months. After the initial run of success there were a few hiccups, but by the end of the season we were playing more like the old United. Our last match of the season was at Maine Road where we had a 4–3 'revenge' win over Manchester City. Matt Busby emphasised the return of an attacking attitude to our play in that match by fielding a forward line of five strikers – Law, Gowling, Charlton, Kidd and Best. George scored two of our goals and Bobby and I got one apiece. It had been a much better season for me with fifteen league goals in twenty-eight league appearances. For my old mate Pat Crerand, though, it was the end of the road. He was sent off in our second to last match of the season at Blackpool. He started the next season under suspension and never again held a regular place in the side. The managers' faces were not all that were changing at Old Trafford. Nobby Stiles would soon be on his way to Middlesbrough, and within two seasons, Best, Charlton and Law would also be gone.

CHAPTER 13

A Stranger at the Helm

Football management is one of the most precarious jobs in the world. It is certainly one of the few where a man can be expected to come straight off the factory floor and start running the company. The price of failure is dismissal, and often humiliation. Wilf McGuinness had not come to the job totally lacking experience, although he may not have had enough of it for the enormous responsibility of taking charge of Manchester United. In choosing his successor, the club decided to go for a person of greater maturity. Frank O'Farrell came to Old Trafford from the manager's job at Leicester City, where he had achieved good results working with limited resources. He brought with him his Filbert Street assistant, Malcolm Musgrove, and at the time it seemed like a good appointment. To men like Matt Busby, success appears to come easily and almost automatically. Others may have their team on the threshold of the championship one moment, then be fighting to avoid relegation within a matter of months. Perhaps this merely illustrates the fine margin between success and failure which there is in all top class sport. At any rate, this was to be United's experience under the new management team.

Because some imbecile had thrown a knife on to the field during a match against Newcastle United, towards the end of the previous season, Old Trafford was closed for our first two home matches of the 1971–72 season. We were ordered to play not less than twenty-five miles away from Manchester, and after genuine away matches at Derby, where we drew 2–2, and Chelsea where we won 3–2, we beat Arsenal 3–1 at Anfield, and then beat West Brom by the same score at Stoke. We had got off to a good start and after losing our sixth match of the season 1–0 at Everton, we were not beaten again until we went down 1–0 at Leeds at the end of October. It was a dream start to the season, and by the turn of the year we had built up a five point lead in the championship race. The goals were going in regularly – George Best had scored 17 and I had notched 12 – everything seemed to be clicking. It appeared that our new management duo had the Midas touch, but even then notable voices were expressing doubt. Such knowledgeable characters as Brian Clough and Malcolm Allison went on record saying that United were in a false position. Allison even went so far as to predict that we would not finish in the top three. Coming from him, with his Manchester City connection, such a remark sounded like jealousy. Certainly all of us thought at the time that he was crazy. Yet his comment proved to be uncannily accurate. In the end we were destined to finish eighth. No sooner had the prophets spoken than the bubble of our successful season burst.

In the end 1972 was to prove a desperate year. On 1 January we went to Upton Park and lost 3–0 to West Ham United. That was then our heaviest defeat of the season and began a remarkable run of seven league defeats for us in a row. After West Ham, we lost to Wolves, Chelsea, West Brom, Newcastle United, Leeds United and Spurs. By far the worst of these results came at Elland Road, a match I missed through injury, where Don Revie's team of reigning league champions thrashed United 5–1, exposing in the process all the flaws in a team which less than two months earlier had appeared to be racing away with the title. I have been asked many times what went wrong over that period, and the short answer is that I just don't know. Clearly our early form was misleading, possibly a carry-over of the successful run which Matt Busby had conjured at the end of the previous season. George Best had performed one of his disappearing acts during January, which couldn't have helped, but it would be absurd to suggest that that alone caused United's slide. Whatever the reason, the reality was that for Frank O'Farrell the winter nights were already closing in.

We had started to concede too many goals and there was clearly a problem in defence. Nobby Stiles and Shay Brennan were gone and hadn't been adequately replaced. Ian Ure had proved a disappointment and was out of the side. We desperately needed a class defender. On the last day of February, O'Farrell bought the young man of the moment when he paid Aberdeen £125,000 for Martin Buchan. Less than a week later he paid Nottingham Forest £200,000 for Ian Storey-Moore in an effort to add something to our striking power. Buchan was a player we badly needed. He was very fast and came down from Scotland with a good reputation. He made his debut at White Hart Lane, where we lost 2–0 to Spurs, but his home debut saw us pick up our first point in eight league matches when we played a goalless draw against Everton in mid-week. That was actually one of the worst games of football that I ever played in, but a point was a point and pretty welcome too by that stage. Ian Storey-Moore, too, was quite fast, and when he got near the penalty box he had a tremendous shot. He had been selected to go to Mexico as a member of

England's World Cup squad in 1970, but had missed the trip through injury. There is no doubt that he was a good player, but I'm not sure that he was ever properly fit from the day he arrived at Old Trafford. He was the only player I ever saw who had to have both ankles strapped up during training. That was surely not a good sign. He actually scored in each of his first three matches for us, but was soon a regular caller for medical treatment. Like so many strikers, he was plagued by knee trouble, which eventually forced him out of the game a few months after joining United.

The arrival of these two new players did help to steady the ship, and there was still a hope that we might salvage something from the season in the FA Cup. We reached the sixth round after beating Southampton, Preston and Middlesbrough, but then went down to Stoke City, after a replay, in spite of having had the initial advantage of being drawn at home. Stoke actually proved to be something of a bogey team to us that season. In November they had beaten us in the fourth round of the League Cup, this time after two replays, and in seven league and cup meetings we managed to beat them only once, 3–0, in our last league match of the season. Finishing eighth in the league meant that after our great start to the season, we had failed even to qualify for Europe. There was nothing to show for a season which had once been so full of promise. Morale had once more started to slip and already our new management team was on the slippery slope to the sack.

Whenever I am asked what it was like playing for Frank O'Farrell, I have to give the same answer, which is that I hardly knew the man. He kept himself remarkably aloof and most of us hardly ever saw him. Although he came down to the Cliff every day, he usually stayed in his office and only came out on Fridays to take the team talk. As I have said many times before – he came a stranger, and left a stranger.

The man we did see plenty of was Malcolm Musgrove, who actually took our training and with whom I got on quite well. There is no doubt that he was very good at his job, and his sessions were much more organised than those we had been used to in the past. They were rather like a military operation, with everything done to the whistle. Where Wilf had made excessive use of the blackboard, Malcolm used the pitch as his blackboard and once again I felt that there was too much planning. Not *as* much, but still to my mind *too* much. Once more I felt that it was a case of worrying too much about the opposition. The theme was 'let's not concede a goal', rather than 'get out and play'. Matt Busby's attitude had always been 'let them worry about us'. Obviously when the opposition got the ball there would be certain key players to pick up, but we all knew the job we had to do without rehearsed moves and being told to stay in a particular area of the pitch.

Within reason Matt had let us do virtually what we wanted to do. If I was told to stay up front that meant I could move around anywhere in the forward line. It didn't mean having to stay precisely in one position. Of course, there were now young lads coming into the team who hadn't the same individual brilliance as some of the players who had played under Busby, but I don't think it helps anybody to try to plan too much. Overall I thought that our training under Malcolm was tough – a bit too tough. Pre-season we did a lot of hard running and I've often thought about modern training that a lot of ability is left on the practice ground. Because it is so tough, by the time they come to play a match, players are often stale and have lost their edge. Whether or not this was what happened to United, I couldn't be sure, but I did feel that our training became a little too 'professional'.

Having ended the season with problems, Frank O'Farrell soon found himself with a few more, in the shape of a wayward George Best. Early in May George went AWOL again, when he failed to turn up to meet the Northern Ireland party who were in Glasgow for a match against Scotland. Then a few days later – one day before his twenty-sixth birthday in fact – George announced from a hotel in Spain that he was 'retiring' from football. Within three weeks he was back at Old Trafford apologising for his conduct and signing a new eight year contract. O'Farrell had ordered him to move out of his luxury home in Bramhall and back to his old digs, in Chorlton, after his walk-out in January. This time it was decided that a cure for Best's problems might be found by getting him to live with Pat Crerand's family in Sale. It was almost the last throw of the dice for George, but it kept him on the straight and narrow for a short while which took us into the 1972–73 season. It was a season which began badly and got steadily worse.

We lost our three opening matches, after which we were in the unaccustomed position of being bottom of the league. It then took us until our tenth league match of the season, on 23 September, to record our first win, when we beat Derby County 3–0 at Old Trafford. In an effort to halt the slide, O'Farrell bought Wyn Davies for £65,000 from Manchester City, and then paid Bournemouth £200,000 for Ted MacDougall. Ted was a prolific goal-scorer, but his scoring had all been done in the lower divisions. Our team was doing badly and it was really expecting too much of either of them to just step in and start scoring goals. It is far easier to step into a good side, as Kenny Dalglish and Trevor Francis have done with Liverpool and Nottingham Forest, and as some of our players did under Busby. It is much more difficult when a team is doing badly. Wyn and Ted both made a modest impact, but the slide continued.

In the League Cup we took two attempts to dispose of third division

Oxford United, then lost at home 2–1 to Bristol Rovers also of the second division. In October, Martin Peters scored his side's four goals as Spurs thrashed us 4–1 at Old Trafford. Then in November, George went 'over the wall' again, and this time he was put on the transfer list. It couldn't go on, and the crunch came in the middle of December, when we met Crystal Palace at Selhurst Park. I was the substitute for that match which turned out to be a humiliating 5–0 defeat at the hands of one of the poorest teams in the first division. That must surely rank as one of United's worst ever results. It left us in twenty-first position in the league and saw the end of Frank O'Farrell's eighteen month reign. Three days later, on 19 December 1972, the inevitable happened. O'Farrell was fired. So too was Malcolm Musgrove and, rather surprisingly, our coach John Aston senior. Under O'Farrell, United had played forty-two league matches, of which we had won ten, drawn eleven and lost twenty-one. It was a depressing record and whoever was to blame, the next manager faced an uphill struggle to get us out of the relegation zone. It appeared too that he was going to have to face it without George Best, because on the day that they announced the dismissal of O'Farrell and company, the club also announced that George would stay on the transfer list and would not again be selected for Manchester United. At the same time, George had himself written to the club apologising yet again for his latest conduct and saying that he did really feel that the time had now come for him to quit. Although he did stage another brief comeback under Tommy Docherty the following season, to all intents and purposes his career with Manchester United was over.

CHAPTER 14

The Axe Falls

I first met Tommy Docherty in 1958. I was eighteen years of age, and Matt Busby had just awarded me my first Scotland cap for the match against Wales, in Cardiff. Docherty had been around the international football scene for several years and was very much one of the senior players. Even in those days he was a bundle of energy – the practical joker in the side. There was never a dull moment when he was around. On the field he was a good strong player – not unlike Dave Mackay – hard in the tackle, but always prepared to take as good as he gave.

Things were very different then on the international scene compared with now. Nowadays there is so much contact between clubs and players, and so much publicity given to the game by press, radio and television, that everyone knows everyone else and a new player coming into an international side is immediately one of the lads. In 1958 it was not at all like that. A young lad like me was virtually an apprentice, and it was rather intimidating to be surrounded by so many seasoned professionals and officials, most of whom were little more than names to me. In the hotel where we stayed, we were naturally expected to be on our best behaviour, and a fresh-faced newcomer certainly wasn't expected to speak. Tommy Docherty and Bobby Collins helped me a great deal at that time by bringing me into the conversation and generally making me feel part of the set-up. They helped me during the game too, which Scotland won 3–0. It was a good debut, and I was even credited with scoring one of the goals, although, as I explained earlier, that was something of a fluke.

Just over a fortnight later I was selected for Scotland again; this time to play against Northern Ireland at Hampden Park. That was a midweek match, and on the Saturday before it I was down in London with Huddersfield Town to play a second division league fixture. Tommy Docherty was with Arsenal at that time, and knowing that I was in town he took the trouble to contact me at our hotel and arranged to take me out to dinner on the Saturday night with a group of his friends. For a young lad who had scarcely been further than Aberdeen and Huddersfield, dining out in London was quite an event and I was very grateful. The following day we travelled together to Glasgow to join up with the rest of the international squad. No one could have done more than Tommy Docherty to make me feel at home in my new international career.

I had reason to be grateful to him again several years later when, in April 1972, he recalled me to the Scotland team at a time when it looked as though my international career was over. I hadn't played in international football for three years when I met him, again in a London hotel, where I was staying with Manchester United on the eve of a league match in the capital. Docherty had taken over managership of the Scotland team six months previously, and was in the process of transforming it from the pathetic joke which it had become, to a force capable of qualifying for the 1974 World Cup Finals. In the eight months before he took over, Scotland had lost to Belgium, Portugal, Northern Ireland, England, Denmark and Russia, and had managed just one draw against Wales. Doc had restored some pride to Scottish football and under his management things had started to improve. When he approached Willie Morgan and myself and asked how we fancied going to Brazil in the summer, to play for Scotland in the mini World Cup, naturally we both said we would be delighted. The following day we learned that we had been selected to play in a friendly match against Peru at the end of the month. It was a great moment for both of us; Willie's only previous cap had been gained against Northern Ireland in 1967, and for me too it was a welcome return from the wilderness. I was even made captain for the match, which we won 2–0, and I celebrated my return by scoring one of our goals.

After Peru, I played in the home international championship before we embarked on the trip to South America. We beat Northern Ireland and Wales, but lost 1–0 to England at Hampden Park and shared the championship with them. This was a distinct improvement on the previous season when Scotland had only managed to take one point from the three matches. The mini World Cup saw us drawn in a group with Yugoslavia, Czechoslovakia and the host nation, Brazil. We drew our first match against Yugoslavia, 2–2, after Willie Morgan had missed a penalty. Then we played a goalless draw with Czechoslovakia before going down 1–0 in our final match to the reigning world champions, Brazil. Once again, although we hadn't actually won anything, Tommy Docherty's revitalised team had given a good account of itself. Our stay in South America lasted about a fortnight in all, during which time Docherty did a first class job keeping the squad in good spirits. There wasn't a great deal of pressure, and he had the knack of making everybody relax. For example, we had initially planned to train at eleven o'clock in the morning, but even during the

Brazilian winter, which it then was, it is hot at that time of the day. We would wake up in the morning to find the sun shining and wouldn't feel too much like training. Docherty would say, 'Fine – no problem – go and have a swim, then get a bit of lunch, and we'll train at four o'clock'. This easygoing approach had a good effect on morale, and the result was that the players were contented and played well in their matches. The training was done, of course, but in a sensible way.

Just as he had been as a player, Tommy Docherty had proved a flamboyant extrovert among managers. He was always in the headlines, and often surrounded by controversy – like the time he sent several of his Chelsea players home from Blackpool for breaking club discipline by being in a night-club when they should have been in bed. As manager of Chelsea, Queen's Park Rangers, Aston Villa, Rotherham United, and Porto, he had experienced both success and failure. He had proved that he could make teams play in the short-term, and had built good sides, particularly at Chelsea, where ironically the man to follow in his footsteps, as he did also at Queen's Park Rangers, was Dave Sexton. But more than once some bizarre incident saw Docherty out of a job and on the move again before his creation had been able to face the test of time. As manager of Scotland it seemed that he had at last settled down – perhaps matured is the right word – and was now beginning to draw on all his years of experience both as player and manager. Certainly Willie Morgan and I returned from Brazil convinced that this was so, which led us to be instrumental in bringing Doc to Old Trafford.

Within five months of our return from South America, Manchester United were in a desperate state of crisis and Frank O'Farrell had been given the sack. When Matt Busby asked Willie and I how we had got on with Docherty and what we thought of him as United's next boss, we both unhesitatingly said that he was the ideal man for the job. He had done wonders for Scotland and was just the man to solve United's management problems. It was in no small way as a result of that conversation that Tommy Docherty became Manchester United's third manager in less than four years. He was appointed on 29 December 1972; three days after Frank O'Farrell had been fired.

When Docherty arrived at Old Trafford, club spirit had reached rock bottom. It was incredible to think that it was less than five years since we had won the European Cup and been at the pinnacle of achievement. Then United had been a perfect club, with perfect management. Everyone, from Mrs Burgess who made the players' tea, right through to the chairman, had been part of one big happy family. Now, after a couple of managerial comings and goings, everything had changed. There was a bad atmosphere about the place. You felt that you had to be careful to whom you spoke, and be guarded in what you said. It was remarkable that things could have changed so much in such a short space of time.

We were faced with the very real prospect of relegation, and that was the new manager's first priority. He set about it in typical swashbuckling style. He has never really changed through the years. Whatever else he may be, Tommy Docherty is a great motivator; particularly of young players. The older ones get to know him quicker, and perhaps see some of his shortcomings, but there is no doubting his immediate impact on any new club. He set about the job at United with his customary enthusiasm, and was soon wheeling and dealing to great effect in the transfer market. George Graham, Alex Forsyth, Jim Holton and Lou Macari were all signed within a short time of his arrival. Graham, Forsyth and Macari had all been on the tour of South America, and with Willie Morgan, Martin Buchan and myself already at the club, it seemed as if our new manager was trying to turn us into Scotland United. He had his own very definite ideas about which were his type of players and which weren't. Frank O'Farrell's most recent big signing, Ted MacDougall, unfortunately wasn't. That was perfectly reasonable. Any manager must have the right to decide which players he wants and which he doesn't. But that does not give him the right to abuse people or to treat them badly.

You have to work closely with someone to get to know them really well. There is a saying that you have to live with a person before you really know what they are like. Before he became manager of Manchester United, my contact with Tommy Docherty had been limited to short spells during international duty. Seeing him on a daily basis, at Old Trafford, showed him in a different light and made me modify my opinion of him. Daily contact with someone at a club is different from occasional contact with a national side. You see and hear things a person is doing every day, and you begin to form a different picture. My impression of Tommy Docherty began to change, so that in time I began to feel that he wasn't quite the fellow I had thought he was. One indisputable fact, though, is that he got United off the floor. Having inherited a situation where we were second from bottom of the league, by the end of the season he had lifted us to eighteenth place and avoided the drop by no fewer than seven points. I can't claim to have had much to do with the revival since I was not a regular member of the side, partly through injury and partly through not being picked. To sustain the sort of improved form which United needed to show at that time, it was essential to keep a reasonably settled side and a player troubled by recurrent injury problems, like mine, would find it hard to establish a regular place. I had also dropped out of the Scotland reckoning again, but I felt that I would be all right once I could get myself back to full fitness. I certainly did not feel that I was anywhere near the end of the road.

One of Docherty's first appointments had been to make Pat Crerand his assistant, which made things a trifle awkward for me. Pat and I had been friends and team mates for ten years and had a regular habit of dining out together with our wives and another couple every Saturday night. When Docherty first came to Manchester he was without his family and was living in an hotel. One Saturday night my wife and I turned up for our regular date with the Crerands and our other friends, and were surprised to find that Pat had invited Docherty to join us. As he was living on his own, I suppose this was reasonable, but it made me feel very uncomfortable. I had nothing against Tommy Docherty personally, but the fact that he was my manager made me feel awkward about sitting down to dine with him. There is nothing wrong with it really, but it's something which doesn't happen much in football and I didn't feel that it looked good. However, there was little that I could do about it, and over the weeks the same thing happened several times. Inevitably our conversation would get on to football, and on at least two occasions, in front of the full group, Docherty said to me that when I had finished playing there would be a job for life for me at Old Trafford. He never specified what the job would be, but I imagined he was referring to a job on the youth coaching side. I had no intention of finishing playing at that time, but it was nevertheless comforting and reassuring to think that when I did hang up my boots, there would be continuity of employment for me at Old Trafford.

I wouldn't be the first that this had happened to: Jack Crompton, Bill Foulkes, John Aston, Wilf McGuinness and Pat Crerand had all done the same thing – and since I had been at the club for eleven years, such a possibility seemed perfectly reasonable. I had been part of Matt Busby's rebuilding after Munich and had helped the club to win various trophies, so why not a place on the staff? I would have liked that. I didn't want to leave Manchester and I didn't fancy being a manager, so a job on the coaching staff sounded fine. It was a nice thought to have at the back of the mind; an ideal way to end my playing career. But it was something which seemed to lie very much in the future, perhaps two or three years ahead. I could hardly be finished as a player, after all it was only six or seven months since I had been a member of Tommy Docherty's own Scotland squad in South America. You can't fall that far in such a short space of time, so there was no way I was thinking of quitting.

As we reached the end of the season, everything in the garden seemed to be rosy. Docherty had been at Old Trafford four months and had steered United away from relegation. There had been one or two comings, and goings, and Bobby Charlton was retiring at the end of the season, but the ship appeared to be stabilising and the immediate future looked reasonably good. For me it was a case of getting back to full fitness, and then things would be absolutely fine. I was completely unprepared for the bombshell which exploded in April 1973.

It was a Friday morning, and United were due to travel down to London to play their final match of the season against Chelsea on the following day. I was not in the team but had taken part in some light training at The Cliff. I was just getting ready to go home when Docherty called me into his office, and utterly shattered my world when he said, 'We've decided to give you a free transfer'. At first I stood there in disbelief. It was the last thing in the world I expected. I could hardly believe my ears. A free transfer! It sounded like a sentence of death. Then the thoughts came crowding in. What about all the promises? What about my wife who was five months pregnant? What about the new house we were moving in to? Docherty knew about these things and had even said that he would get the club to give me a mortgage. What about the promise of a job for life? After all his big talk, he was now telling me that I was *out* of a job. I couldn't believe it. I felt as if I had been stabbed in the back.

As I quickly gathered my thoughts I realised that my most immediate concern was that the news shouldn't come out. I was afraid that it might upset Di, and I certainly didn't want to end my career like that – discarded. I felt that I still had two or three seasons left in top class football, but my exit now seemed to be a *fait accompli*. I certainly didn't want to leave Manchester, where my children were at school and my family was happy. On the other hand, I had no intention of playing football in a lower division, and the only other first division club around was Manchester City. The idea that I might wind up there seemed so unlikely that it didn't even occur to me. One or two of United's older players had gone to Stoke in the past, but I didn't fancy that, so there was only one thing for it. I didn't want to leave Old Trafford, but if United no longer wanted me, then I would quit.

I was due to have a testimonial match against Ajax, at Old Trafford, in the first month of the following season, so I suggested to Docherty that I should use the occasion to announce my retirement. My contract still had a year to run, so it would be in the club's interests for me to do that. I would have the testimonial match, then I would quit the game. That way the club would be spared the expense of settling the outstanding part of my contract, and I could go out of the game at the top. It would also spare me the pain of having to upset my wife, and give me a little time to sort out my plans. The benefits to both parties were obvious; it was an easy way out for him, and the perfect way out for me. 'Yes, that sounds terrific!' he said. So it was agreed; in return for my assurance that I would announce my retirement immediately after my testimonial match, he promised that there would be no more talk of a free transfer. After the intial shock of being told that I was no longer wanted, it was at least some relief to know that I had managed to arrange for a more dignified end to my career than the one Docherty had had in mind for me.

My children were spending the Easter holidays in Scotland and I was due to go to collect them the following day. In the circumstances, I said to him: 'My kids are in Scotland, you don't mind if I go up there to collect them, do you?' He said, 'No, you go up and get your family back. After the match against Chelsea we're off to Italy to play in the Anglo-Italian tournament. See me when we get back in about ten days time. In the meantime we'll leave it like that.' And that was how it was left. Because I was confident in my mind that I had reached a mutually satisfactory agreement with him, I said nothing to Di about what had happened. Nor did I mention it to any of my family and friends in Scotland when I got there. I told no one. There was no point, since nothing was supposed to come out about it until the start of the next season. I thought that I had given him the easy way out.

I left Di at home in Manchester, and set off for Scotland alone. I was reliving the whole thing in my mind as I drove, and remembering the promises made over those Saturday night dinners: promises which obviously hadn't been worth a light. As far as my playing career was concerned, I had always known that the time would come. All right, players have to go when their time is up, but I had always felt that when my time came I would know without being told. I couldn't accept that my time really was up, but there was nothing very much I could do about it. As I wasn't prepared to move either to another town or a lower division, then that seemed to be that. I was still trying to sort out my private thoughts when the second bombshell landed the following day.

At lunchtime on the Saturday, I was in a pub in Aberdeen, having a drink with some friends. There was the usual noisy babble of voices and clatter of glasses and we were watching the football preview programme on television. It had just been announced that Arsenal were asking £25,000 for Frank McLintock to go to Queen's Park Rangers, and we were in the middle of discussing that, when suddenly up came my photograph and the news that Tony Dunne and I were being given free transfers by United. There was a deathly silence. I was speechless. How could he have done that after we had agreed to leave it until next season? I sat there absolutely stunned, not knowing what to say to my friends. Why hadn't I told them? What could I say? If I said I hadn't known about it I would look a fool; if I *had* known about it then why hadn't I said something? Whatever I said I was going to look stupid. I muttered something about not wanting to upset anyone and rushed back to my sister's. Within an hour the family home was under siege as the nation's press and television descended upon us. My family too wanted to know why I hadn't said anything; it was a nightmare. Di, of course, was still on her own in Manchester. By now she too would be knee-deep in reporters, and she hadn't known anything about it. I had to get home. The following day I piled the kids into the car and set off back to Manchester.

As I was racing back down the M6, I had plenty of time to think. I couldn't understand why Docherty had done it. Apart from the simple matter of having given me his promise, I couldn't see what he had to gain. I thought that I had offered him the perfect solution. He had given me his word, then gone behind my back. All that he was getting this way was publicity, which was going to cost the club money. It was inexplicable. One thought above all others occupied my mind: the fact that what had happened could never be changed. It was too late now to do anything about it. I had been given a free transfer and there was no going back from that position. There was no way that the club could turn round and change their minds. There was no way now that I could turn round and say 'Fine, I'll stay on until the beginning of the season and retire after my testimonial'. All of that had gone. Whether I liked it or not, I was being thrown out with the washing-up water. The worst aspect of it was that he did what he did without warning me. I was on the telephone in Aberdeen and the club had my number. Whatever Docherty's reasons were for breaking his promise, he could at least have let me know. Then I could have prepared my wife and family for the shock. No one can dispute a manager's right to pick and choose the players he wants. All right, if he didn't fancy me that was his prerogative, but there are surely ways and ways of going about things.

When I returned to Manchester I went to see Sir Matt that same evening to see if he could explain what had happened. He told me that it was 'pressure from the media, in London' which had forced Docherty to release the news. That explanation wasn't worth two bob, of course, because according to Docherty's agreement with me there should have been no news to release.

Apart from my close family and friends, I never mentioned anything to anybody at the time about the background to these events. No one knew about the private deal which Docherty and I had made. To the public at large I had been given a 'free', and that was all there was to it.

The story only became public when I was due to appear in court in 1979 to give evidence on Willie Morgan's behalf in a libel case which Docherty was bringing against him for remarks he had made during a television programme. I was not particularly looking forward to having to appear on the stand, and give evidence, so I was quite relieved when Docherty admitted that everything which had been reported about my case in court was true. It saved me from what I feel would have been an ordeal. After all, I wasn't suing anybody for damages and no one was suing me. I was only going to appear reluctantly to keep faith with Willie Morgan. Since the story became public, people have asked me if I bear Docherty a grudge because of what happened, and the answer is that I don't. Of course, I was very upset about it at the time, and for several months afterwards, but I think if a person carries a grudge indefinitely then there is something wrong with the person himself. I would certainly not want to have any dealings with Docherty, and on the occasions we have met since, our conversation has been limited to a polite hello, although I suspect that he might have been prepared to carry on as if nothing had happened had I let him. What he did to me was unforgivable, but I soon got over it. What I can never forgive him for is what he did to my family.

CHAPTER 15

My Life's Ambition Fulfilled

Six days after Tommy Docherty had first told me that I was being given a free transfer, I attended the Football Writers' Association dinner in London. I felt that my career as a professional footballer was over, and I had no idea what I was going to do with my life. Since the news of my free transfer had become public, a number of offers had been made on the telephone, but nothing at all which interested me. Had someone said to me at that moment that I would appear in another Wembley final, then go on to achieve my life's ambition by representing Scotland in the World Cup Finals, I would have said they were mad. Yet these were just some of the things which did happen to me in my last remarkable year in football. I was also destined to play under three different managers, and score the goal which appeared at the time to have relegated my old club, Manchester United.

Also at the FWA dinner was Johnny Hart, who had recently taken over managership of Manchester City, following the departure of Malcolm Allison. Before we sat down for the meal, Johnny asked me if I had made any plans, and when I said that I hadn't, he asked me how I fancied going back to Maine Road? His question came right out of the blue: it represented an incredible turn around of events after what had happened to me at the weekend. There was absolutely nothing to think about: if City wanted me back, then I would go. We shook hands on it then, and during the close-season the formalities were completed so that when the curtain rose on the 1973–74 season – which was to be my last – I was back in a Manchester City shirt.

Starting my second spell as a Manchester City player, I felt as if I had been given a new lease of life. It was a great feeling and I got off to a cracking start with two goals in our 3–1 win over Birmingham City, on the opening day of the season. A week later I scored again in a 1–1 draw at Stoke. Three goals in eight days was not bad going for someone who was supposed to have been on the scrap-heap. It was great to be back.

Suddenly the whole pattern and outlook of my life had changed. Just a few months earlier my career had appeared to be finished, now it all seemed to be on the up and up. My good start to the season had caught the attention of the new Scotland team manager, Willie Ormond, who came to Maine Road to watch our league match against Coventry City. Willie was a good friend of my great buddy Ken Barnes and, although he said nothing to me, he told Ken that I would be in the Scotland team for the vital World Cup qualifying match against Czechoslovakia towards the end of September. Naturally enough, Ken told me, so that I knew about it before it was officially announced. There had been some talk in the papers that I might be brought back for this make or break match for the benefit of my experience, but I hadn't really believed it, and so I was both surprised and delighted by the news. Soon after I had been selected for Scotland, I got a knock playing for City and spent several anxious days getting myself fit. Because of that I went to the international match without having played for Manchester City during the previous fortnight.

Scotland were drawn in World Cup qualifying group eight, along with Denmark and Czechoslovakia. They had already beaten Denmark twice during Docherty's reign, and since the Danes had also taken a point from Czechoslovakia – whom we still had to play twice – the position was clear. We needed two points to qualify: if we could beat Czechoslovakia in our first encounter, at Hampden, then Scotland would be through to the World Cup Finals. On the night of 26 September 1973 there were 100,000 people crammed inside Hampden Park for what, for the Scots, was to be a night of destiny. The atmosphere was a crackle of anticipation, but the noise was dramatically turned into deathly silence when Nehoda put Czechoslovakia ahead early in the game. Suddenly there was a strange eeriness about Hampden Park. Jim Holton brought us back into the game with an equaliser before half-time, but although we were pressing continually, the second goal just wouldn't come, as the second half began to run out. Then, with just fifteen minutes to go, Willie Ormond decided to make a substitution: he sent on Joe Jordan in place of Kenny Dalglish. Within two or three minutes of stepping on to the field, Jordan had headed the goal which took Scotland through to the World Cup Finals for the first time since 1958. The celebrations in Glasgow that night must have resembled VE day. When I got back to Manchester after playing in the international match, I found that I was still out of the City side for their next league match against Burnley. Such are the ups and downs of a footballer's life.

For me, September had been a memorable month, and it ended on a high note when, on the thirtieth, my wife Di gave birth to our daughter Diana – our first girl after four boys. Now the Law 'team' was really complete.

In October I went to Bratislava to play for Scotland in the return game against Czechoslovakia. The result, of course, was academic and after a very physical match they beat us 1–0 to gain some measure of revenge. The same night, England failed in their bid to beat Poland at Wembley, which meant that they were out of the competition. Scotland would be Britain's only representative in the 1974 World Cup Finals. Since 1966, the wheel had turned full circle.

In November 1973 Manchester City were forced to appoint a new manager when Johnny Hart had to retire because of illness. The man chosen to succeed him was the former boss of Norwich City, Ron Saunders, who came to Maine Road with the reputation of being a bit of a hard man. Tony Book, who had ended his playing career only a few weeks earlier, was appointed his assistant.

A new regime meant a new approach, and once again I found myself playing to a system which didn't really suit me. Under Johnny Hart's management, our coaching was handled by Ken Barnes whose whole philosophy of football was based on attack – short, quick balls, and one-twos. Ron brought in an entirely different approach. As had happened at Old Trafford under Wilf McGuinness and Frank O'Farrell, the emphasis shifted to a more defence-orientated outlook and Ken Barnes took a bit of a back seat as the pattern of our game was changed. Ron Saunders was a good professional, very enthusiastic about the game and very conscious of fitness. His training was varied, but it was more to do with hard work than ball work. Instead of trying to capitalise on the flair of players like Francis Lee, Rodney Marsh and Mike Summerbee, he preferred a more methodical approach. He appeared to take delight in calling some of the older players *old* players, which some of them didn't like. It was said as a joke, but I always felt there was a bit of seriousness behind it.

Ron Saunders was at Maine Road for five months and his main achievement in that time was to get us to the League Cup Final, which we lost 2–1 to Wolves. I was injured in the semi-final first leg against Plymouth, and was out of the side until the week before we went to Wembley. Even then I was not really fully fit, and neither were Rodney Marsh and Francis Lee, who were both struggling with knee problems. All three of us played in the final, but our condition must have shown in our play which was not terribly good. By then the City side wasn't quite what it had been a couple of seasons earlier, and perhaps there was some justification in Saunders' remarks about age. The club had had its best period between 1968 and 1970, winning four major trophies in three seasons. Now, although they were still a good side, they were on the decline. The poor performance in the League Cup Final was a reflection of league form, and by the time Ron Saunders went, at the beginning of April, we were too close for comfort to the bottom of the first division. The only solace for City players at that time was that Manchester United were in an even worse position.

One week after losing the League Cup Final we were given a bit of a roasting by Leeds United, although the score was actually only 1–0. Rodney Marsh, Francis Lee and I were all dropped after that match and once again my career was reaching a crisis point. A couple of weeks later I was horrified to learn that a fourth division club was interested in signing me and Saunders was clearly all set to sell me if I agreed. I was playing in the reserves at the time which was no place to be at my age, and had that been all there was in the future I would have quit there and then. But we were just a few months away from the World Cup Finals, and I had set my heart on winning a place in the Scotland squad. My prospects of doing that were not good while I was in the reserves, and they would not be improved by a move to a lower division, so I said to Saunders that I preferred to stay where I was and fight to get back into the first team. I was still not completely fit, but I set out on a desperate drive to get myself back into contention before the end of the season. Eventually I was recalled to the first team for the match against Queen's Park Rangers at the beginning of April. Ironically, that was virtually Ron Saunders's last act as manager of Manchester City. We lost the match 3–0 and the following day he was sacked.

That highlights one of the tragedies of football. Ron then went to Aston Villa where he is doing a successful job, so who's to say what went wrong at Maine Road? Perhaps he came at the wrong time. Managers tend to join a club at a time when things are going badly, and it is particularly hard to join in mid-season when the pattern is already established. City were not doing well when he joined us, and when a team is doing badly confidence goes and it is very difficult to get it back. Any manager has in mind what he feels is the right way to go about building the team. He's expecting to be there for a few years and should try to make changes gradually. For what it is worth, my own feeling is that Ron tried to change things too quickly. His departure left Tony Book in the manager's chair, and with four matches to play our immediate concern was to reach a position of safety in the league. We achieved this when we beat West Ham United, 2–1, at home in our second to last match of the season.

Although I didn't realise it at the time, my last match of the 1973–74 season was to be my very last match in league football, and by an amazing coincidence it was the Manchester 'derby' at Old Trafford. City had mathematically guaranteed their first division survival the previous Saturday, but United were still very much in the throes of relegation trouble and it was one of life's incredible ironies that I scored the goal which at the time appeared to have sent them down. Actually, they would have gone down anyway, since both Birmingham City and Southampton, their fellow strugglers, were winning their final matches of the season. No one at Old Trafford knew that though when, with only minutes of the match remaining, I back-heeled the ball past Alex Stepney into United's net, for the only goal of the match. I was standing with my back to goal when the ball came across from the wing and it was really no more than a reflex action which made me flick out my heel as it went past.

I didn't realise until I saw the incident on television film, years later, how close I had been standing to the centre of the goalmouth, and of course, it was one of those situations where more often than not I would have failed to make contact. On this occasion though I made perfect contact, and the ball went into the net like an arrow for a goal which at any other time I would have been proud of. As it was I felt sick. I have seldom felt so depressed in my life as I did that weekend. After nineteen years of giving everything I had to score goals, I had finally scored one which I almost wished I hadn't. I'm sure that a lot of people thought at the time that I would be pleased about it, in view of the way I had been treated by United the previous year, but nothing could be further from the truth. I had spent eleven years of my life at Old Trafford, and although I had been upset by what had happened to me, most of the people there were still my friends. It was like having been at a firm for eleven years where I had had some great times and knew the people intimately. All right, things hadn't gone too well at the end, but that didn't mean that I bore a grudge; life is hard enough without that, and I certainly didn't want to put the final nail in their coffin.

The truth was that I hadn't even wanted to play in the match, and although I never actually asked to be left out, I did have a long chat about it with Tony Book. In the end though, we decided that as a professional it was my job to play, even though I might not be looking forward to it. I had a responsibility to City, and Tony was trying to get his team playing well after a fairly wretched season. Professionally I was glad we had won, but deep down I was not too happy. Soon after I had scored there was that infamous pitch invasion which caused referee Mr David Smith to abandon the match eight minutes early, but of course the Football League quite rightly ruled in the circumstances that the result should stand.

Having had a reasonably successful end to the season, I was bang in the reckoning for international honours. After I had got over my initial shock at what had happened at Old Trafford, my thoughts turned to the home international matches which were being played the following week. In May I had equalled George Young's record of fifty-three appearances for Scotland, when I played in the match against West Germany in Frankfurt. I needed one more appearance to create a new record, but more than that of course a good performance or two in the home internationals would go a long way to securing my place in Willie Ormond's World Cup squad. I got my fifty-fourth cap in the first of our three matches, which was against Northern Ireland at Hampden Park. It wasn't a very good performance either by me or the team, and we lost 1–0. I wasn't too surprised, therefore, at being left out of our next match against Wales, but I was disappointed to find that I wasn't even named as one of the five substitutes. The team played well in that match, so I was not expecting to be picked for the match against England on the Saturday, but I did hope that I might at least be a substitute this time. Once again though, I was left out, and I began to think that my chance had gone out of the window. The World Cup squad was due to be announced on the Monday morning, and I was on tenterhooks all over the weekend. Thankfully my fears were unfounded. I was in the Manchester City dressing room, with Willie Donachie, when the news came through that, with the sole exception of Jim Smith of Newcastle, Willie Ormond had named all the players who had taken part in the home internationals in his World Cup squad. I was on my way to Germany!

Although I played in only one of our three matches, playing for Scotland in the World Cup had to be the greatest thrill of my football life. It was also a fitting climax to my career. I didn't plan it that way, but the match against Zaire was my very last first-class match. It always seems that one is looking for excuses, but I really do think that Scotland were unlucky to have to play Zaire in their opening match. They were very much the unknown quantity in our group, and although they were obviously the outsiders, it was going to be goals scored against them which would decide who qualified in the end. As much homework as could be done had been done, but there was still a great deal that was unknown about Zaire. No one expected them to be up to the standard of a top European or South American side, but no team reaches the finals of the World Cup without having something – remember how North Korea beat Italy in 1966. We knew that Zaire were supposed to have one or two decent players, and we were determined to be on our guard.

For all of us, this was our first ever experience of playing in World Cup Finals, and the simple business of standing through the playing of national anthems was a nerve racking and energy sapping experience.

We desperately wanted to do well, but were rather afraid to express ourselves for fear that something would go wrong. As it was we got what we thought was a reasonable 2–0 victory, after hitting the woodwork a couple of times and having several efforts cleared off the goal line. Unfortunately we got a rather bad press after that match which I think affected the team in our next two matches, against Brazil and Yugoslavia. I thought that personally I had done reasonably well, and although I was disappointed at not having scored I felt sharp and was really feeling like playing. I imagined that we would keep the same side for the match against Brazil, and I never even thought about being dropped, so I was particularly disappointed when I learned that I had lost my place to Willie Morgan. That was great for Willie, but to compete with the best you have to score goals and I think Willie would be the first to admit that he is not a potential goal-scorer.

To draw 0–0 with the reigning world champions was a great result for Scotland in one way, but I really thought that we should have beaten them. Brazil weren't half the side that they had been and they had become very physical, perhaps as a result of their experience when they were literally kicked out of the tournament in England in 1966. Coming back to Europe eight years later they seemed to have decided that that was the way to play it, and I was very disappointed to see that they played the same way again in Argentina in 1978. In 1974 they were there to be taken, and I felt that with Billy Bremner controlling the game, as he did, Scotland should have won. However, we didn't, and on the same day Yugoslavia thrashed Zaire to the tune of 9–0. As Brazil and Yugoslavia had already played out a goalless draw, that meant that Scotland now had only two ways to qualify for the final eight. Either we must beat Yugoslavia in our final match, or we would have to hope that Brazil failed to beat Zaire by a margin of three goals. Being realistic, after what Yugoslavia had done to Zaire, we couldn't really hope for the latter alternative, which meant that our real task was to beat Yugoslavia. That being the case, we would have to score goals and I therefore thought there was a fair chance that I would be back in the team – but to my great disappointment Willie Ormond kept an unchanged side.

Once again Scotland had plenty of domination, but again our play lacked real penetration. It's all very well knocking balls up into the box, but there has to be someone there to put them away. All that Scotland could manage was a 1–1 draw, which wasn't enough. For a while there was a hope that we might still go through to the final stage as Brazil surprisingly struggled to get the three goals they needed against Zaire. The third one finally went in just eleven minutes from the end of the match, and Scotland were out of the World Cup without having lost a match. We were the only team in the tournament to remain unbeaten – even the eventual winners, West Germany, lost one match to their neighbours East Germany. Willie Ormond was delighted by his team's performance, and I suppose he had every right to be, but I was a little disappointed because I felt that we should have done better. We certainly should have scored more than two goals against Zaire and I think that we would have done so had it not been our first match. I also thought that we might have beaten both Yugoslavia and Brazil, so it was with mixed feelings that I returned home. I was upset that we hadn't done better, and yet I was delighted to have achieved my ambition of playing for Scotland in the World Cup Finals. With that experience behind me there wasn't much left to accomplish in the game.

At the start of the 1974–75 season I found that there was no place for me in the Manchester City team, and I realised that I had at last reached the end of the road. I still had a year of my contract to run and Tony Book wanted me to play in the reserves, but I didn't fancy it. He even suggested that I might take things easy and play only in reserve matches at home, but I could see no point to that. If I was being asked to help young players, then perhaps I might have felt that I had a job to do, some sort of role, but simply to play in the reserves at that stage of my career was something I couldn't face. I wouldn't have done it under Ron Saunders, the previous season, without the incentive of trying to get back into the reckoning so that I might play in the World Cup. Now there was no such incentive, and there appeared to be no future.

I had always been determined that I would get out of the game at the top, and I could see now that my time had come. I had had nineteen fabulous years during which I had done more or less everything that there was to do. Now it was time to call it a day. I slept on it for a couple of nights, then on August Bank Holiday Monday 1974, I announced my immediate retirement. My career as a professional footballer was finally over.

CHAPTER 16

The State of the Game

I have often been asked why I didn't stay in the game when I retired. Why, for instance, I didn't want to become a manager. Of course offers were made at the time to play in other countries, such as Ireland, Australia, Norway, Holland, South Africa, Scotland, and America. Had I retired four or five years later than I did, then I probably would have gone to America; by then, the sort of money which was being offered, not to mention the numerous 'fringe benefits' (such as cars, houses and lucrative advertising contracts), had increased tremendously.

Players now can go to the States and ensure financial security for themselves and their families for the rest of their lives. Increasing numbers of our top players are doing this, and I think that the drain will continue. At first the Americans were mainly interested in big name players who had retired from the game, such as Pele and George Best. Now they are turning their attention towards top players who are still playing, and people like Franz Beckenbauer, Johan Cruyff, Johan Neeskens, Gerd Muller and Denis Tueart, have found the temptation of the massive rewards and the good life too great to resist. Most of the British players who have been attracted, like Trevor Francis, try to combine playing in America with playing in Britain, but I wonder how long it will be before there is a real exodus of top British talent? In 1974 the sort of offers being made to me were quite generous but for a five month season were insufficient to tempt me, considering the upheaval and the problem of finding work and an income for the other seven months of the year. Looking back now, I'm inclined to think that I retired a few years too soon.

I never fancied a career in football management. Some people are cut out to be managers, others are not, and I didn't really feel that I was. As I've said already, I wouldn't have minded a job in some sort of coaching capacity, working with young players, but none was being offered at the time I retired. I've often felt that sufficient use isn't made of the knowledge and experience of retired players, too many of whom are allowed to drift out of the game after they have finished playing. Football is one of the few industries where a man who has had a working life which has taken him from rock bottom to the very highest levels of his trade, going through every phase and experience of the job on the way, can then be discarded at around thirty-five years of age, just when he is in a position to be putting something back into the game. In business and industry, the exact opposite happens. Experienced people are used to train and encourage the new and the inexperienced. You can see, for example, how someone like Bobby Charlton could be in charge of an area of, say, Manchester, looking after schoolboys, visiting clubs and schools, passing on his vast experience. At the moment this sort of thing is done by schoolteachers and FA coaches, most of whom no one has ever heard of, and none of whom, to my knowledge, has ever achieved anything significant in the game.

Although a few do go into management, and some join the coaching staffs of clubs, the majority of great and very good players tend to leave the game when they have finished playing because there is nothing for them to do. It is clear that some drastic rethinking is required if this situation is to be changed. I suspect that the same thing happens in sports other than football too, but I am convinced that the game would benefit considerably if a real effort was made to tap this great reservoir of knowledge which at present is just being allowed to go to waste.

The British game is at the moment facing some quite serious problems. For one thing, there is a general decline in the quality of football being played and a real absence of skilled players. Apart from people like Kenny Dalglish and Liam Brady, there are few outstanding players around and with the exception of the top three or four teams, the overall standard of play is mediocre. There is also the threat of a talent drain to Europe and America – although steps have been taken recently to curtail the loaning of players – which, hand in hand with the whole thorny question of escalating transfer fees, highlights a growing financial crisis.

When Trevor Francis was sold to Nottingham Forest and became the first £1,000,000 footballer, the deal set a new scale of rates for transfer fees, just as each successive increased fee has done over recent years. This inflationary spiral can only end in disaster unless it is stopped, because there just isn't sufficient money in football to support it. In the end it is the banks who will win, while more and more clubs will find themselves in dire financial straits, with some of them probably forced to go out of business. Already the number of clubs who actually expect to come to the end of a season breaking even, or just making a profit, is down to a few. The vast majority are losing money hand over fist. One problem is that the revenue gathered at the turnstiles doesn't match the money spent on transfers and other expenses. Spanish and Italian clubs can quite gaily pay out huge sums for players because the cost of watching football in those countries is many times higher than it is in Britain. Therefore a large transfer fee has much more chance of being recovered in income.

It also seems to me that there are far too many professional clubs in the English League, with the result that the whole of the game's resources, both players and money, are spread too thinly. For instance, a smaller first division would mean a greater concentration of talent and result in players having fewer matches, and therefore a much less arduous season. With fewer, but stronger teams, the matches which were played would generally be more attractive and the public could reasonably be asked to pay more to see them. Perhaps in time the economic forces I have mentioned might bring these sort of changes about; like the case of supermarkets and little shops, the little shops will have to go. Until that happens, though, the football authorities show no sign of changing things for themselves. The reason for that, I suppose, is that no one wants to give up his particular foothold in the game, and by and large it is the lame ducks who resist the sort of surgery which would ultimately produce a much smaller but healthier patient.

On the question of escalating transfer fees, I think it is a great pity that the clubs wouldn't accept the system put forward a couple of seasons ago by Cliff Lloyd, whereby a fee would be calculated according to a player's age and the wage that he had negotiated with his club. Such a scheme would clearly relate the club's expenditure to its income, and it also had a built-in provision for scaling up or down transfer fees between clubs in different divisions. For instance, a first division club might be asked to pay ten times a player's annual wage, a second division club six times, and so on. It would not only have been seen to be scrupulously fair, but more important it would have put a brake on the transfer inflation which now seems to have got totally out of hand.

Whatever the economic facts of life, there is no doubt in my mind that the football being played today is far less attractive than it was ten or twelve years ago. The game is desperately short of star players and I believe that there are two basic reasons for this. Changes in social standards mean that youngsters are not developing their natural skills in the way that they did when I was a lad, and those lads who do finally wind up in professional clubs often find that modern coaching is forcing them into a mould rather than allowing individuality to flourish. In Scotland we used to refer to someone who had good ball skills as a 'tanner ball player'. Those skills were invariably developed in the streets, at an early age, where kids with nothing else to distract them played for hours on end with a ball. This wasn't the case just in Scotland, it happened across the world. Pele, Eusebio, George Best, and many others all had the one thing in common. They came from poor backgrounds and spent their childhood playing football, morning, noon and night. I did the same thing myself, and none of us learned our trade out of a manual or a text book. You don't see kids playing so much street football nowadays. The first thing that most of them do when they get home from school is to switch on the television. They all have some programme or other that they want to watch and it doesn't leave much time for football. When I was a lad we didn't have television.

While I was in Argentina during the summer of 1978, I was fascinated to see an exhibition of incredible ball skills performed by teenagers from various parts of the world. They were taking part in a competition staged during the World Cup Finals, and quite honestly some of them could do things with a football which would put many of our modern players to shame. The youngster who eventually won the competition did so by keeping a ball in the air with over two hundred and fifty flicks. I heard at the time that a senior FA coach who was also present was extremely critical of the event, describing it as a 'nauseating spectacle which had nothing to do with football'. This to me highlights an attitude which is the root cause of many of the problems of the modern game. No one would suggest that being able to juggle a ball means that a lad is going to make a footballer. But surely ability like that must be a great asset to any kid who really wants to become a player, and it's much better to have skill like that than not have it. I'm appalled today at the number of players who can't trap or head a ball properly; who can't pull a ball down or slow the game down; who can't create anything. The game seems to be based on destroying rather than creating. The great virtue now seems to be being fit and able to run. If you have these attributes you have a chance of becoming a player. Skill seems to have been forgotten.

A little over a decade ago, coaches were unheard of in Britain. We've always had a trainer; players have to train and be fit and practise ball skills and so on, but since the middle sixties, we've had this new breed of football person – the coach. Coaches are much more concerned with tactics and organisation and over recent years they have become very important people indeed, and yet I think they have done a great deal to stifle skill. The emphasis is on method rather than developing natural talent. It's a problem which not only affects *professional* football, but one which has gone right to the grass roots. I remember when I was a lad that the woodwork teacher took our football at school. He did it because he liked football, and because he enjoyed looking after the kids. He never attempted to coach us or tell us how to play. We'd just get twenty-two players on the pitch and go at it like bees round a honey jar. There was plenty of time for introducing a little method when we were older. Nowadays in schools there is usually someone who looks after the football who is probably just as keen as the woodwork teacher, but because there is so much talk about coaching he tries to instil it into the kids. Youngsters are told not to come over the halfway line, or to stay in a certain area of the pitch. They are being forced into moulds instead of being allowed to develop their skills naturally. When they get to a club they often find it is the same there, so that by the time they are seventeen they are programmed like robots but haven't mastered the basic skills of the game. These to me are the products of a great deal of modern coaching, and what puzzles me is how we got into this position. How is it that coaches have become so powerful, what have they ever achieved?

The four most successful British managers during the bulk of my playing career were Bill Shankly, Matt Busby, Bill Nicholson and Jock Stein. With Liverpool, Manchester United, Spurs and Celtic, the four of them built a number of great sides and won just about everything there was to win. Their teams played the most entertaining and skilful football, and each of them won a major European competition. Yet these were not managers noted for being committed to the coaching philosophy. When you look at those four names and their records and realise that they didn't have this coaching bug, and didn't try to force players into moulds, you wonder what is going on. Their achievements were based on playing attacking, not defensive, football. You have to defend when you are being attacked, of course. But basically, they made the opposition worry about their team rather than the other way around. Today, Bob Paisley and Brian Clough are setting the pace, and neither of them is noted for being too heavily committed to the use of coaching manuals either.

A couple of seasons ago, when Don Revie went off into the desert, two of the six candidates for the job of England Manager were Alan Wade and Charles Hughes, two of the most senior people in the FA coaching scheme. Yet I feel sure that if you had asked around the game, the majority of players would not have known who they were. I'm not saying that coaching is a bad thing, we need coaching to a point, but I am saying that the emphasis on it has got out of hand.

I played professional football for nineteen years, from schoolboy level to the very heights of the game, and when I hear some of these coaches talking, as I have done through the years, I just don't know what they are talking about. If theirs is the right way, then the game I played was not football. Two coaching expressions which became fashionable in football towards the end of my career used to leave me wondering what the game was all about. One was 'work-rate'. It sounded to me as though someone was talking about a horse. Two of the best players I ever saw, Jimmy Greaves and Ferenc Puskas, had nil work-rate, but where are their equals today? Not being produced by any coaching scheme, that's for sure. Another phrase which I often hear, and wonder about, is used when a manager has bought a new player. He might say, 'He'll do a good job for me'. I always think that that sounds as if the fellow is going to be building walls instead of playing football. Whatever happened to that simple game I used to play as a kid? My old pal Pat Crerand once came out with a marvellous quote which for me sums the whole thing up beautifully. He said, 'If one day all the tacticians reached perfection, the result would be a 0–0 draw – and there would be nobody there to see it'. I couldn't possibly put it better.

We saw in the 1978 World Cup Finals how many of the matches were reduced to the spectacle of a game of chess. The importance of winning has become too great and nobody smiles any more on the pitch. Teams are far more concerned about picking up opposition players than about creating chances, so the decline in entertainment value in football is a worldwide problem, not just a British one. Fortunately, the final itself was contested between the two highest scoring teams in the tournament, so perhaps there is hope. Argentina were probably the best attacking side in the competition, although they had one of the worst defences and I doubt if they would have won the Cup had they not been playing at home. Holland, on the other hand, were superb. Apart from some rather uncharacteristic physical stuff in the first twenty minutes or so of the final, they were a joy to watch. They had an excellent blend of solidity in defence and great skill in attack. They showed tremendous variety in their play, including the ability to score spectacular goals from long range.

For me, as for all Scotsmen, the big disappointment of Argentina 1978 was Scotland's failure to reach the last eight of the competition. What made it worse in a way was the feeling that we really should have qualified. After dismal performances against Peru and Iran, the brilliant 3–2 win over Holland – the eventual losing finalists – surely demonstrated Scotland's true potential and confirmed that they should have reached the last eight. I've always believed that the hardest thing about the World Cup is actually qualifying for the Finals, which is something England have failed to do twice in succession, so in that respect simply getting to Argentina was a significant achievement for a small country like Scotland. Having got there it was a great pity that we did less well in the competition than we should have done. It was a great opportunity lost. On the financial side Scottish football benefited by nearly a quarter of a million pounds as a result of the three matches which Scotland did play. That figure would probably have been doubled had they reached the last eight, which would have helped to provide many badly needed facilities at all levels of the game in Scotland. More though than money, I feel that our players lost a marvellous opportunity to gain experience of playing football at the very highest level, which is what they need if Scotland hope to maintain a position among the major soccer nations.

Since Argentina, the great soccer debate in Scotland has been on why we failed to do better. Many words have been spoken on the subject and I was particularly interested to hear the views of the former Brazilian official, José Bonetti, who was general manager to the team which won the World Cup in Mexico, in 1970. Speaking in Scotland recently, where he was attending a managers' get-together, he said that before the 1978 World Cup Finals began Scotland had been one of the teams feared by the South Americans. They had been on a successful tour of Chile, Brazil and Argentina the previous summer, and were thought by the South Americans to be a strong side likely to do very well; even perhaps to reach the last four. I believe that he put his finger on the real reason for our failure when he suggested that it was due to a lack of preparation. The British game still suffers from a strange misguided belief that, with a few notable exceptions, the rest of the world doesn't really know much about playing football. We tend to imagine at both club and international level that many of the teams from overseas are still a bit amateur in their outlook and likely to be fairly easy pickings, when in fact most of them are extremely professional and take things very seriously indeed.

When Scotland were drawn in the same group as Holland, Peru and Iran, I was appalled at the way almost everyone in Britain seemed to assume that that gave us automatic qualification for the last eight, along with Holland. I had played against Peru in 1972, and although we had beaten them 2–0, at Hampden Park, it was obvious then that they could play a bit. But despite having had that experience, and despite the fact that in 1978 they would be playing under South American conditions, the thinking seemed to be that Peru were an ageing side who were going through a bad spell and that they would be a bit of a pushover. I believe that too little was done actually to find out about their strengths and weaknesses, with the result that Scotland went into that vital match ignorant of Peru's capabilities and therefore underestimating them.

One of the biggest problems that players face on a long trip is boredom. To give their best on the field they have to be in the best possible mental, as well as physical, condition. Morale plays a vitally important part on these occasions and it is essential that players should be made to feel comfortable. They should have nothing to worry about except playing. I believe that the art is to make things as near normal as possible. Scotland's accommodation at Alta Gracia was something of a photographer's paradise: externally the hotel and its setting were beautiful. Unfortunately, the same was not true of the interior where the rooms were drab and uninviting and there was little in the way of comforts or entertainment. To be fair, it had been promised that there would be a swimming pool in the grounds, but it wasn't completed. Because of the tight security, the players were virtually imprisoned in the hotel grounds – which meant that apart from the relief of morning training sessions and playing in three matches, they were shut up for a fortnight with very little to do.

From what I saw personally it seemed to me that although the administrative arrangements for Scotland's trip to Argentina were in many ways better than they had been for Germany four years earlier, there is still a fair way to go to reach the standard which is essential if we are to compete successfully in major international tournaments. I believe that many valuable lessons have been learned from Argentina and that the professionalism of modern international football is now better appreciated in Scotland. If this is so then what happened in Argentina could in the long run prove to be a blessing in disguise.

Before we can put into practice what we have learned, though, Scotland must first qualify for another major tournament. In the long term our sights will be set on the World Cup Finals in Spain in 1982. Before that there is the European Nations Cup in Italy, in 1980, for which England are already as good as qualified. Scotland's position is less hopeful since we have lost our two opening matches but the position is not hopeless. The luck has not been going Scotland's way too much in the short time since Jock Stein again took over as manager, but these things take time. There is no more able or ex-perienced manager in Scotland than Jock, and I am absolutely con-fident that in the long run things will work out for him. Three of our four remaining Nations Cup qualifying matches are at Hampden Park and although our position may look bad at the moment I have a sneaking suspicion that Scotland will pull it off. Failure to do so will not be the end of the world, but the experience our players could gain by going to Italy would be invaluable, with the long term objective of the Spanish World Cup Finals in mind. The chance is there for the team which Jock Stein is building to take a bold step along the road to confirming Scotland as a major name in international football.

Appendix: Career Record 1956-57 to 1973-74

LEAGUE CAREER

Joined Huddersfield Town as a groundstaff apprentice in **April 1955,** and signed professional forms for the club on **25 February 1957.**

On **15 March 1960,** transferred from Huddersfield to Manchester City for £55,000 – a new British record transfer fee.

On **9 June 1961** transferred from Manchester City to Torino (Italy) for £110,000 – a record fee between British and Italian clubs.

On **12 July 1962** transferred from Torino to Manchester United for £115,000 – a new British record transfer fee.

On **2 July 1973** free transfer from Manchester United to Manchester City.

Retired **August 1974.**

INTERNATIONAL APPEARANCES FOR SCOTLAND

Date	Opponent	Venue	Score	Goals
1958				
18 October	Wales	Cardiff	3–0	1
5 November	Northern Ireland	Hampden	2–2	—
1959				
27 May	Holland	Amsterdam	2–1	—
3 June	Portugal	Lisbon	0–1	—
3 October	Northern Ireland	Belfast	4–0	—
14 November	Wales	Hampden	1–1	—
1960				
9 April	England	Hampden	1–1	—
4 May	Poland	Hampden	2–3	1
29 May	Austria	Vienna	1–4	—
9 November	Northern Ireland	Hampden	5–2	1
1961				
15 April	England	Wembley	3–9	—
26 September	Czechoslovakia	Hampden	3–2	2
29 November	Czechoslovakia	Brussels	2–4	—
1962				
14 April	England	Hampden	2–0	—
20 October	Wales	Cardiff	3–2	1
7 November	Northern Ireland	Hampden	5–1	4
1963				
6 April	England	Wembley	2–1	—
8 May	Austria	Hampden	4–1	2
4 June	Norway	Bergen	3–4	3
9 June	Eire	Dublin	0–1	—
13 June	Spain	Madrid	6–2	1
7 November	Norway	Hampden	6–1	4
20 November	Wales	Hampden	2–1	1
1964				
11 April	England	Hampden	1–0	—
12 May	West Germany	Hanover	2–2	—
3 October	Wales	Cardiff	2–3	—
21 October	Finland	Hampden	3–1	1
25 November	Northern Ireland	Hampden	3–2	—

1965

10 April	England	Wembley	2–2	1
8 May	Spain	Hampden	0–0	—
23 May	Poland	Chorzow	1–1	1
27 May	Finland	Helsinki	2–1	—
2 October	Northern Ireland	Belfast	2–3	—
13 October	Poland	Hampden	1–2	—

1966

2 April	England	Hampden	3–4	1
22 October	Wales	Cardiff	1–1	1

1967

15 April	England	Wembley	3–2	1
10 May	Russia	Hampden	0–2	—
21 October	Northern Ireland	Belfast	0–1	—

1968

6 November	Austria	Hampden	2–1	1

1969

16 April	West Germany	Hampden	1–1	—
6 May	Northern Ireland	Hampden	1–1	—

1972

26 April	Peru	Hampden	2–0	1
20 May	Northern Ireland	Hampden	2–0	1
24 May	Wales	Hampden	1–0	—
27 May	England	Hampden	0–1	—
29 June	Yugoslavia	Belo Horizonte	2–2	—
2 July	Czechoslovakia	Porto Alegre	0–0	—
5 July	Brazil	Rio De Janeiro	0–1	—

1973

26 September	Czechoslovakia	Hampden	2–1	—
17 October	Czechoslovakia	Bratislava	0–1	—
14 November	West Germany	Hampden	1–1	—

1974

27 March	West Germany	Frankfurt	1–2	—
11 May	Northern Ireland	Hampden	0–1	—
14 June	Zaire	Dortmund	2–0	—

Total appearances 55
Total number of goals for Scotland 30 – a record for Scottish International
Football.

Denis Law

CLUB PLAYING RECORD

Season	League Appearances	Goals	FA Cup Appearances	Goals	League Cup Appearances	Goals
Huddersfield Town						
1956–57	13	2	5	1		
1957–58	18	5	2	1		
1958–59	26	2	—	—		
1959–60	24	7	3	1		
Manchester City						
1959–60	7	2	—	—		
1960–61	37	19	4	2*	2	—
Manchester United						
1962–63	38	23	6	6		
1963–64	30	30	6	9		
1964–65	36	28	6	3		
1965–66	33	15	7	6		
1966–67	36	23	2	2		
1967–68	23	7	1	0		
1968–69	30	14	6	7		
1969–70	10	2	0	0	3	1
1970–71	28	15	2	0	4	1
1971–72	32	13	7	0	2	0
1972–73	9	1	1	0	2	2
Manchester City						
1973–74	22	9	1	2	3	1
Totals	**452**	**217**	**59**	**40****	**16**	**5**
In Italy – Torino						
1961–62	27	10				

* *Figures do not include six goals scored in an abandoned cup-tie when playing for Manchester City against Luton Town.*
** *Competition record.*

174

EUROPEAN PLAYING RECORD

Manchester United

	European Cup		European Cup-Winner's Cup		Inter-Cities Fairs Cup	
	Appearances	Goals	Appearances	Goals	Appearances	Goals
1963–64	—	—	5	6	—	—
1964–65	—	—	—	—	10	8
1965–66	8	3	—	—	—	—
1966–67	—	—	—	—	—	—
1967–68	3	2	—	—	—	—
1969–70	7	9	—	—	—	—
Totals	**18**	**14†**	**5**	**6**	**10**	**8**

† *Club record for the competition.*